Street Connect: His-story

From the depths of addiction to a movement of hope

By Ricky McAddock

malcolm down

PUBLISHING

Endorsements

'In Psalm 113 God is described as stooping down to lift the poor from the dust and the needy from the ashes. In this book you will find a fascinating description of how God does this. From the rescue and transformation of one man's life into a national ministry that is stooping to reach many for God's sake. This is not a story of self-help but an account of what amazing things can be accomplished when someone is willing to walk by faith, one step at a time. I'm sure this book will inspire hope in many who read it to trust the same faithful God that Ricky and Julie have.'

Phil Hills, Chief Executive, Teen Challenge UK, and Vice-President, Global Teen Challenge

'This is an immensely moving and inspiring story of amazing grace, transformation and formation. It's an intimate insight into the birth, beginnings and establishment of one of the kingdom's most valuable and powerful ministries among broken and disenfranchised people. Street Connect is growing in its reach and influence across this nation because of its roots in amazing grace. Ricky's life, testimony, and example are witness to the power of the gospel of Jesus Christ. What God has done for Ricky, God can do for you.'

Ivan Parker, National Leader, Apostolic Church UK

'This is a wonderful story of God's amazing grace. It is the gripping account of a life being rescued and redeemed, then repurposed to bring hope and help to others. I am so inspired by Ricky's leadership and excited to see many more chapters unfold.'

Tim Morfin OBE, Founder and Chief Executive, Transforming Lives for Good (TLG)

'This is a story of raw hope and abounding grace. Ricky's honesty shines through every page; gritty, courageous, and full of the redemptive power of God. From the depths of addiction to the calling of leadership, his journey captures the soul of a nation in need of healing, and the God who steps in. This book will inspire, challenge, and lift your eyes to what's possible through Jesus – a testimony our churches and communities must hear.'

Alasdair Bennett, Chief Executive, Bethany Christian Trust

'Ricky's story is both deeply personal and yet universal – the drive to survive, the seduction of cool, the numbing balm of intoxication for an inexpressible emptiness and pain. It is the story of a Borderland warrior and survivor who journeys through deconstruction to reconstruction, trading ashes for beauty. Ricky perfectly embodies sharp intellect, deep spirituality, street-toughness, and entrepreneurial instinct, resulting in the impactful ministry Street Connect, which he co-founded with his equally powerful wife, Julie. If you sense you are being called towards something more, read this book and get to it! Inspirational.'

Charles Maasz, Chief Executive, Glasgow City Mission

'Ricky's is the ultimate story from despair and near death through to fulfilling a calling to help countless people caught in addiction across the country. From a troubled and painful childhood, to finding faith, beating addiction, and going on to start and build Street Connect with Julie, his life story is fast paced, humbling and inspiring. Highly recommended for anyone in need of hope that they should persevere to find their God-given purpose in life!'

Mark Kitson, Associate Director, Cinnamon Network

'Wow! From the first page the raw, brutal honesty of Ricky's descent into near-fatal addiction and his initial struggles to break free bring into violent clarity the chaotic lives of so many hurting, desperate people. The contrast with the eternal call of a loving Father who never gives up on us is striking – a beautiful thread weaving through Ricky's story, Julie's story and the story of all the lives turned around through the work of Street Connect. This is a powerful story of redemption, reconciliation, obedience, God's faithfulness, the key role of local church and of the power of God's love to transform society – and it is not over yet! Every church leader needs to read this!'

Alistair Barton, Director, Pray for Scotland, and Chair, Street Connect Board

First published 2026 by Malcolm Down Publishing
www.malcolmdown.co.uk

29 28 27 26 25   7 6 5 4 3 2 1

British Library Cataloguing in Publication Data
A catalogue record for this book is available from the British Library.

ISBN 978-1-917455-48-0

Cover design by Nick Amis
Art direction by Sarah Grace

Printed in the UK

Typeface: The Grace Typeface® by 2K Denmark

Dedication

FOR MY MUM

You never gave up on me, loved me unconditionally, and cheered me on through every season.

Your sudden passing meant you never got to read this book, but your voice, your strength, and your love echo through every page of this story.

This book is for you.

Disclaimer

This book is based on the author's real-life experiences. To protect privacy, the names and identifying details of some individuals and locations have been changed. While every effort has been made to preserve accuracy, certain conversations have been recreated or adapted to reflect the essence of what was said. In some cases, the contributions of multiple people have been combined into a single exchange for narrative flow and readability. These adjustments have been made with care to remain faithful to the heart and truth of the experiences shared.

Contents

Foreword

I first met Ricky in 2019, and from the outset I sensed the unmistakable fingerprints of God on his life – his heart for the church, for the most marginalised, and for the expansion of God's Kingdom, not his own.

There was something about him – the honesty, the humility, the rawness of his journey – that gripped me. His story is one of the most powerful I've encountered: from the depths of addiction, shame, and brokenness to the founding of a ministry that now brings hope to the very people he once walked among.

As the founder of Christians Against Poverty, and more recently i61m, I've had the privilege of journeying with many who've faced enormous personal battles. What stands out in Ricky and Julie's life is the way they've experienced grace – not just to be forgiven, but to be propelled forward so that others might receive that same grace too.

This book is more than an amazing story. It's a testimony – a powerful reflection of God's faithfulness to pursue, rescue, and rebuild. Ricky didn't just find freedom – he discovered a calling. And in discovering that calling, he and Julie began to live out the truth that God uses ordinary people for extraordinary purposes.

Their story resonates deeply with Lizzie and me. It's been a joy to walk alongside them over these past few years. I've had the honour of being a friend to Ricky – encouraging and supporting him. He's been so open to the things I've learnt over the last 30 years, and yet I always see that he's seeking and hearing from God for himself in every decision.

What you'll read in these pages is the fruit of deep surrender, inner healing, and the refining work of the Holy Spirit. Ricky's story reminds us that leadership is forged in the hidden place – often through pain – and that the most authentic leaders are those who've been led through the wilderness by the Good Shepherd himself.

Ricky's transformation has been extraordinary. Seeing him grow in his sensitivity to the Spirit of God has been inspiring. He is strategic and driven, yet repeatedly lets go of his own plans in obedience to God's leading. The Lord is shaping a life that is already influencing many – and will go on to impact many more.

Today, Ricky and Julie's story is bringing hope to some of the most vulnerable people in our society. Their charity, Street Connect, is a living example of the gospel in action. But more than that, they are living proof that no life is beyond the redeeming power of Christ to change, and no past is beyond being used for his glory.

So, if you're wondering whether God still has a plan for you – if your failures, addictions, or pain have made you feel disqualified – this book is for you. May it awaken hope, stir faith, and remind you, as it reminded me, that God's grace reaches deeper than we could ever imagine.

Dr John Kirkby CBE
Founder of Christians Against Poverty and i61m

Prologue

The Ashfield Road Hotel

'Wake up!'
'Wake up, please.'
He kept yelling – frantic, desperate – 'Wake up! Wake up!'
'Get up!'
'Come on!'

Matt's voice rang out in my ears as I drifted back into consciousness. His words pierced through the fog in jagged fragments.

Where was I?
What had he done?
What had I done?

***

'Wake up!' came the voice again – louder this time, panicked and relentless – but it wasn't coming from Matt standing beside me now.

It was coming from the phone in his hand.

'Watch this,' he muttered, breathless and pale, shoving the screen towards me. 'You need to see.'

I blinked and tried to focus. Matt had stopped shouting. But the phone was playing a video, and in that video, he was in full-blown panic.

Just another cold, miserable night in the East End of London – but colder still was the state of my soul.

The grand-sounding Ashfield Road Hotel was nothing more than a holding pen for the forgotten. Its once-brown carpet was scorched with cigarette burns. Grimy white walls bore streaks of tea stains left by occupants long gone. The lingering stench of stale smoke clung to everything, like a second skin.

Though I tried to shut my eyes to the mess, the place was a multisensory indictment – a living, breathing reminder of just how far life had spiralled.

This wasn't a hotel. It was a 21st-century throwback to the Dickensian shadows of Victorian London.

Less a place to rest, more a drag-net catching those already sinking through society's cracks.

I had arrived just weeks before, unravelling again. Christmas had come and gone in a blur of smoke and silence. And now, here I was – waking up to something worse than the place itself.

***

On screen, Matt's voice was wild with fear.

'Wake up!' he screamed. 'Please, come on, lad!'

The video trembled as he tried to rouse someone lying motionless on the bed.

'No, no – not another one,' he muttered between frantic breaths. 'Please, I've done my time. Not again.'

I stared, unable to look away. The skin was waxy, pale. Lips tinged blue. The figure wasn't moving.

'Look!' Matt's voice shouted again through the phone, even as his real-life self stood frozen beside me, no longer yelling – just watching me carefully, watching for a reaction.

The room in the video.
The angle.
The light.
The familiar stains on the wall.

That's this room.
The bed . . . was this bed.

I didn't say a word. But Matt saw it in my face.

***

His muttering started – barely audible, more to himself than to me.

'Not my fault . . . just trying to help. This ain't the same. I didn't leave nobody. Not this time.'

He paced, rubbing the back of his neck, twitching, blinking.

'Didn't hide nobody,' he whispered. 'Didn't put no one nowhere. Not again.'

Then he glanced at me, eyes wide.

'I just did what I could, yeah? Had to do something.'

There was a pause. His hand was still holding the phone, the image frozen now on a still frame of the pale figure – lifeless, lips blue, silence hanging heavy.

'Wasn't like before,' he added quietly. 'That was different. That weren't my fault either.'

He wouldn't meet my eyes.

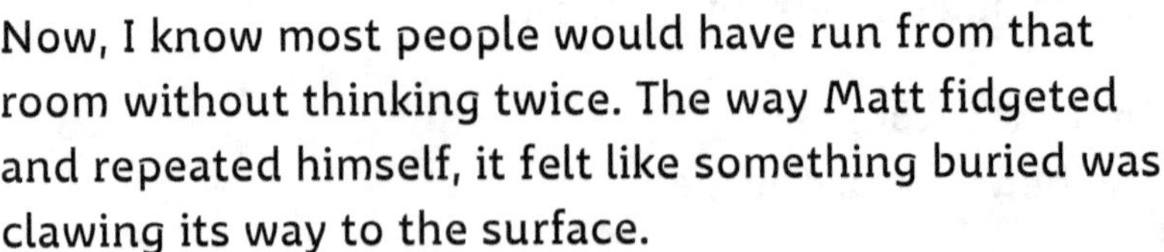

Now, I know most people would have run from that room without thinking twice. The way Matt fidgeted and repeated himself, it felt like something buried was clawing its way to the surface.

But I stayed.
Because something darker than fear had its grip on me.

That's what this kind of life does – it partners with danger, makes a home with risk, marries treachery. It numbs out reason and replaces it with craving.

And so, instead of running, I sat there.
Watching.
Listening.
Letting the horror settle.

He stared at me.
I stared at the phone.

And something in the air told me this wasn't over.

Chapter 1

Formative Years

Teribus ye teri-odin! roared the riders, their ancient war cry tearing through the black border night like a blade. The air itself seemed to tremble as the sons of Hawick rose from the shadows – not as soldiers, but as avengers.

Onwards! shouted the gallant youth, their hastily mustered steeds pounding a dreadful rhythm into the blood-soaked soil beneath them – earth long scarred by the struggle between two neighbouring nations.

On, lads, on!

It was the year 1514. Scotland was still reeling from the slaughter at Flodden Field the year before. In Hawick, not a single man between sixteen and sixty was said to have survived. And so, it was left to the sons left behind to defend their town.

They surged across the Scots' March with fire in their hearts, determined to halt the raiding party that had spilled across the border – burning, looting, and desecrating what little remained. They rode not for conquest, but to protect their kin. These were no seasoned warriors, but boys shaped by grief – burning with the memory of the fathers they had lost.

In the English camp, the first signs of dread came not from the men, but the animals. Tethered horses reared and snorted, the trembling of the ground felt through their hooves before the ears of men caught the sound. Pack animals twisted in panic. Dogs fell silent, sensing the shift in the air.

The English had grown careless. There were no sentries, no perimeter. Their confidence bred vulnerability. They assumed they had broken the back of border resistance. After all, hadn't the Scots lost their king, their nobles, and most of their fighting men in a single day?

And yet, it is often in the ashes that something fierce begins to grow.

***

The thunder grew louder.

Then, it struck.

In a flash of raw brilliance, the Hawick youth had driven a herd of cattle into a funnel, sending them stampeding through the camp. Horns and hooves tore through tents and men alike. What followed was a storm of mud, blood, and steel.

Behind the chaos rode the boys – not battle-hardened soldiers, but sons, grieving, burning, wild with purpose.

The English were caught off guard. Their numbers meant little in the dark, in the confusion, in the face of those who had nothing left to lose.

And then came the final blow – the youth of Hawick captured the English standard.

A stunning reversal. A message sent.
It was a humiliation, yes – but more than that, it was redemption.
Not just for the town, but for those who had been left behind.
Fatherless and forgotten . . . but not finished.
They had risen.
And they had prevailed. A victory for the little guy.

***

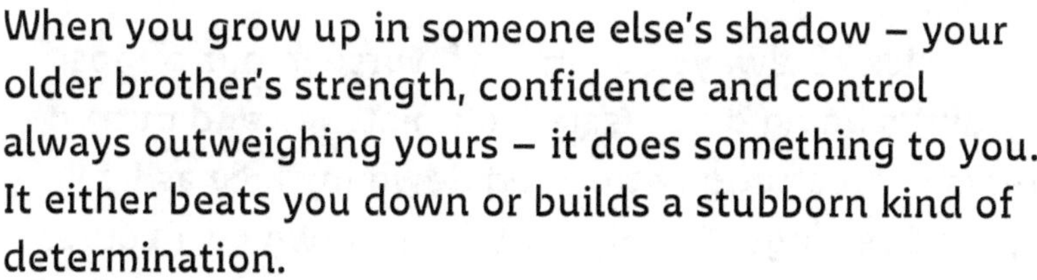

When you grow up in someone else's shadow – your older brother's strength, confidence and control always outweighing yours – it does something to you. It either beats you down or builds a stubborn kind of determination.

That's why the Hornshole story still resonates with me.[1] In the face of overwhelming odds, it was the young, the underestimated, who rose and overcame. That kind of grit has a way of shaping how you see yourself.

It might help explain how Scotland has so often punched above its weight on the world stage – contributing to science, engineering, philosophy and medicine at a rate few countries can rival. Inspiration, innovation and determination seem to define our national mindset. Maybe struggle and progress are inseparable.

I've certainly found that to be true.

So it was for me. Not so much sharing a border as sharing a bedroom – conflict with my stronger, older brother was inevitable. And, like those boys of Hawick, I'd have to get creative to stand my ground.

***

I was going to get him back for this.
This time, he was going to pay.

I was sick of always coming off worse in our scraps – always being outmuscled, outmatched and outrun. Tears of frustration streamed down my face as I plotted revenge. My big brother was two years older

1. 'The Battle of Hornshole', *Hawick Common Riding* – Official website: https://www.hawickcommonriding.co.uk/history/hornshole (accessed August 2025).

than me – an advantage that felt enormous back then. He was taller, stronger, quicker. But I had something else: a plan.

He'd be watching TV on the sofa, relaxed and unaware. I just needed to time the ambush perfectly – or things could go very wrong. If I gave him a chance to react, I'd be the one needing rescue.

So I waited. Watched. Then, like a commando on a covert mission, I crawled into position. Stealth mode activated.

My heart thudded in my chest as I crept behind the couch. This was it. My moment.

I sprang to my feet like a bowstring released, wound up a mighty left hook – and crack! – landed it clean on his face.

Time to run.

I sprinted out of the living room and straight into Mum's bed. It was early on a Saturday, and she was enjoying a well-earned lie-in after a hard week at work. My timing couldn't have been better.

He was raging, chasing me down, but I'd already launched phase two of the plan: the Mum shield. Hearing the commotion and my panicked cries, she leapt into action. I was under the covers, playing the innocent. My brother was furious. Mum was having none of it.

He got a full scolding from her – and a black eye from me.
A proper *keeker*, as we say in Scotland.
For once, I'd come out on top.

And whatever retribution he might've planned later . . .
it was worth it.

***

The homes and hearths of Hawick were once the beating heart of a thriving woollen mill industry. But by the time I arrived on the scene in 1979, that heart was already beginning to slow. Our charming little Border town still held its pride, but decline had begun to creep in.

That same year, Margaret Thatcher became the first female Prime Minister of the UK. Love her or loathe her, she left a mark. And she certainly left one on Hawick – quite literally – when she visited on 4th September 1986.

'You're the kiss of death, Maggie!' someone shouted as the motorcade passed through the town. Her husband Denis was met with a flying egg – an image that would go down in local folklore. Whether it was protest, performance or just mischief, it summed up the atmosphere of the times: unsettled, uncertain, and full of strong opinions.

Across the UK, Cortinas, Orions, Novas and Maestros cruised the roads. In homes, shoulder pads grew, hi-fis boomed, and Rubik's Cubes twisted under frustrated fingers. Thatcher's economic policies were reshaping the country – mines were closing, strikes were growing, and unemployment was climbing. But at the time, all of that was just background noise to me.

Hawick remained the centre of my world.

Across the pond, Reagan had entered the White House. The Cold War was heating up. Diana and Charles were stoking a royal obsession. Britain had gone to war with Argentina. The world was bracing itself for HIV and AIDS.

But I wasn't thinking about any of that.

I was more focused on who I'd be fighting at school that week – and dreaming of one day scoring the winning goal in the Scottish Cup Final.

***

Growing up in the Scottish Borders during the 1980s, in a single-parent home, was all I knew. We lived in a small two-bedroom flat in Burnfoot – the roughest council estate in the area. Hawick itself was surrounded by breath-taking countryside, and on the surface it looked idyllic. But underneath, a different reality had begun to take hold.

Burnfoot, once thriving, began to fray. Opportunities dried up. Families struggled. Eventually, it was ranked among the 10 per cent most deprived areas in Scotland – a label that stuck, even to this day.[2]

But to me, it was simply home.

Despite the challenges of the area, our flat was kept to a high standard. My mum worked hard to make it that way. She was the glue that held everything together – a strong, determined woman who had started in the woollen mills at just sixteen. She often spoke about the 'good old days', when you could leave a job in the morning and walk into another that same afternoon. Even as the mills declined and the town changed, she did everything in her power to provide for us.

And she did it well.

We never went without, and she even managed to take us on several holidays – including a few trips to Spain that I've never forgotten. If she struggled, we rarely saw it. If she went without, it was never obvious. She made sacrifices behind the scenes, always making sure we had what we needed.

I didn't see the stigma or the statistics attached to Burnfoot – I saw my wee world. The place I played, fought, laughed, and grew. And at the heart of it all was my mum. She created a sense of security and

2. Scottish Government, *Scottish Index of Multiple Deprivation (SIMD) 2020*, https://www.gov.scot/collections/scottish-index-of-multiple-deprivation-2020/ (accessed August 2025).

stability that allowed me to feel safe, cared for, and free to just be a boy.

It wasn't until years later that I realised how much she carried on her shoulders – and how quietly she bore the weight.

***

My dad moved to Hawick from Glasgow as a teenager, after my grandad came for the fishing and fell in love with the town's Common-Riding festival and the horses. He and my mum met in their teens – full of energy and passion. They married young, before life had really taught them what lasting commitment would require. Two boys came along in quick succession. Later, we all moved to Glasgow for Dad's work, but after a short spell, my mum returned to Hawick, and, soon after, the relationship came to an end.

I have no memory of them being together. And growing up, life without a dad in the house just felt normal. A lot of my friends were in the same boat.

Not long after the separation, Dad took a job in the Middle East – the shorter of two stints abroad. After returning to Scotland, he remarried, took on his new wife's two children, and later they had one of their own. When I was twelve, he headed back to the Middle East for a second, longer stretch that lasted more than eight years.

Both he and my grandad were tough Glaswegian men – hard-working, strict, and unbending in their standards. And in some ways, I was relieved not to have that constant pressure around. Mum was softer, more forgiving. I got away with more under her watch. But as I got older, I began to realise how much I missed a father's consistent presence in the home. His guidance. His protection. His authority.

At the time, I didn't think I was missing anything. But you don't miss what you've never known – until you start to see what you needed.

Over time, I began to understand that the breakdown of the family unit leaves more than just a gap at the dinner table – it leaves quiet wounds. I've come to see how growing up without a father in the home can shape a boy's sense of identity, security, and self-worth. This isn't about blame – far from it. It's about naming the gap. Recognising the subtle ache that comes from the absence of certain voices, examples, and steady hands.

When one parent carries everything alone – even when they do it with grace and grit, like my mum did – something is still missing.

The bigger picture confirms this. The majority of runaways, behavioural disorders, and those in prison come from father-absent homes.[3] These aren't just

3. David Blankenhorn, *Fatherless America: Confronting Our Most Urgent Social Problem* (New York: Harper, 1995).

statistics – they're stories. Struggles. And in many ways, they reflect parts of my own.

I wasn't consciously angry back then. But looking back, I can see the signs. My temper flared easily. I fought a lot – at school, at home, especially with my older brother. There was a restlessness in me I couldn't explain. And at the root of it all was a quiet ache. A father-shaped space that no one else could fill.

But I don't blame my dad. And I certainly don't blame my mum. They were young. Life can be tough. They did the best they could with what they had – while carrying wounds of their own, like we all do. I can see that more clearly now.

Whatever their struggles, they gave me life. And much of who I've become is because of them.

For that, I'll always be grateful.

As I moved into my teenage years, something began to shift.

Insecurity crept in – quiet at first, like a shadow at the edge of the room. It's a familiar story for many lads that age: trying to figure out who you are, where you fit, and how to carry yourself when your confidence hasn't quite caught up.

I found my early fix in alcohol.

It started innocently enough – a few cans of cider or lager before heading to the local youth club. It made me feel more relaxed, more confident. Less like the awkward teenager, more like someone who could hold his own.

But that feeling didn't last. And before long, I was chasing stronger stuff – cheap fortified wine, anything that could take the edge off. These weren't just drinks. They were masks. Armour. A shortcut to the version of me I thought people liked more.

By the time I was a couple of years into my teens, alcohol wasn't enough. I started smoking cannabis, then dabbling in amphetamines. The crowds changed. The nights blurred. My edges began to fray.

At the time, though, it all felt normal.

It felt like freedom.

That's when Liam came into my life.

He was a couple of years older and completely different from anyone I'd known. Sharp, streetwise, unpredictable. If I had to compare him to an animal, he was a weasel – quick, slippery, always working an angle. He'd moved to Hawick from Manchester and brought with him an edge that most of us didn't have. The local police already knew his name. Most parents warned their kids to stay away. But to some of us, he was magnetic.

Liam had a way of making chaos look cool.

'Ricky! You were wild last night! What was that all about?' he laughed, clapping a hand on my shoulder.

'Which bit you on about?' I replied, trying to mask the blank spaces in my memory.

He grinned. 'That punch you threw – one hit and he went down! What a belter!'

Fragments started floating back. Flashes of shouting, laughing, fists flying. My stomach twisted slightly, but I forced a smile. Better to laugh along than show any weakness.

'Did you actually take all those diazepam tablets?' another lad asked.

'Yeah . . . I think so,' I said, remembering how I'd washed down a handful with cheap Buckfast wine.

It was reckless, but in that moment I didn't care. Mixing tranquillisers and drink had become part of the ritual. They numbed everything – the insecurity, the overthinking, the guilt I didn't yet have words for. They let me feel untouchable.

At least until the cannabis kicked in. Then came the wave of nausea, cold sweats, and dizziness. I ended up in the bathroom, being violently sick. If that happened to someone, they'd be fair game for ridicule for days. Beneath the laughs, though, I was starting to lose myself.

Nights blurred together in a cocktail of alcohol, pills, and smoke. I'd wake up full of regret, piecing together patchy memories – but instead of changing course, I kept going.

I didn't know it then, but I was already drifting far from the boy I used to be.

And I was just getting started.

As the years rolled on, so did the chaos.

My run-ins with the police became more frequent – fights, possession, being in the wrong place at the wrong time. I was showing up in court more often than my family liked. It was no longer just teenage rebellion. The choices I was making were beginning to shape my future in ways I didn't yet understand.

By 17, I had fallen in with a new crowd – a couple of lads from Edinburgh. They were about the same age as me but were already into harder stuff. With them, I crossed a line I'd always said I wouldn't.

'Fancy trying something that'll blow your mind, mate?' one of them grinned, his voice soaked in mischief.

'What is it?' I asked, already knowing it wasn't going to be good.

'It's heroin.'

I hesitated. 'Ach, I'm no sure. You got any Valium?'

'Naw,' he scoffed. 'This is better. Way better. Just try it.'

He turned to my girlfriend. 'You got any tinfoil?'

'Aye, I'll get some,' she said, heading to the kitchen.

A few minutes later, I watched them 'chase the dragon' – heating the heroin on foil and inhaling the smoke through a makeshift straw. Their eyes softened, their faces melting into quiet euphoria. It looked peaceful. Powerful. I felt curiosity tighten its grip.

'Why not?' I muttered. 'Give me a shot, then.'

He handed me the straw. 'Don't waste the smoke.'

I mimicked what I'd seen – dragging the brown line across the foil, inhaling deeply.

The effect was immediate.

A dizzy wave crashed over me. My skin prickled. My stomach flipped.

'He's gonna be sick!' one of them laughed as I bolted for the toilet, heaving into the pan.

Between retches I gasped, 'What is this stuff? I hate it. Give me drink and Valium any day – they give a much better hit.'

I thought that would be the end of it. I stuck to that mix for the next few years. But heroin had already entered my story.

And it wasn't done with me yet.

***

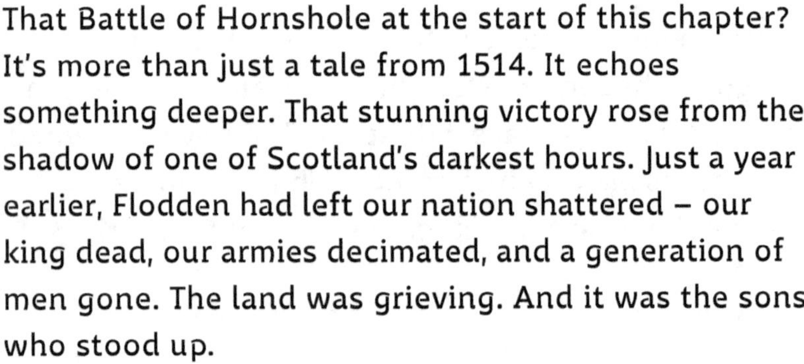

That Battle of Hornshole at the start of this chapter? It's more than just a tale from 1514. It echoes something deeper. That stunning victory rose from the shadow of one of Scotland's darkest hours. Just a year earlier, Flodden had left our nation shattered – our king dead, our armies decimated, and a generation of men gone. The land was grieving. And it was the sons who stood up.

I see echoes of that story in my own journey. Not because I was without love or care – far from it. My mum was a rock. She carried more than her share with grace, grit, and fierce determination. And my dad, though not always present, still shaped parts of who I became. But like many boys growing up without a consistent father figure at home, I had to find my way through questions I didn't yet know how to ask – about who I was, how to be strong, and what it meant to become a man.

Those boys of Hawick didn't wait for permission to rise. They rode out in the dark with what they had – courage, conviction, and the memory of those they'd lost. In their own way, they turned pain into purpose.

I wasn't on horseback, and my battles weren't fought with steel. But the war inside me was just as real. Addiction would soon cross the borders of my life like an invading force, and I'd be left with choices: to run, to surrender, or to rise.

But not yet.

For now, I was still charging blind – restless, reckless, and full of fire.

Still unaware of just how many opportunities would be missed before I was ready to rise.

Chapter 2

Missed Opportunities

Opportunity favours the bold.

It's a lesson I've learned through both success and failure – that when you've got the drive to go after what's in your heart, and the courage to act on it, doors begin to open. As Sun Tzu once said, opportunities multiply as they are taken.[4] And from a young age, I felt that drive burning inside me. Even as a boy growing up in Hawick, I sensed there was more to life than what I could see. More to explore. More to become. I didn't have the language for it then, but I felt the pull of something bigger – like the world was calling me beyond the boundaries of my small town.

Later, I came to understand the difference between destiny and fate. Destiny is something you chase; fate is something you accept. One is active, the other passive. As the philosopher Martin Buber put it,

---

4. Sun Tzu, *The Art of War*, translated by Lionel Giles (1910).

destiny is achieved, fate is received.[5] I didn't want to be someone who just drifted into a life I never chose. I wanted to shape my own story.

But as you'll see in the pages ahead, destiny and fate don't always stay in their lanes. Sometimes they blur – entwined like a double-edged sword, where ambition opens one door and disaster another. And sometimes, they look so similar it's hard to tell which one you're walking through until it's too late.

Even as a kid, I felt the tension. I'd look down on the town from the hills above imagining it expanding – more buildings, more jobs, more chances to grow. But deep down, I knew the real change I longed for wasn't about Hawick getting bigger. It was about me getting out.

That hunger only grew stronger through my teenage years. I didn't just *want* more – I *needed* it. Bigger cities, new places, a different way of life. I was wired for adventure, fuelled by ambition, and already reaching for something beyond what I could yet hold.

I'll never forget the first time I visited Dubai.

I was fifteen, away on holiday with my stepmum and my siblings from Dad's side. Even then, Dubai felt like

5. Martin Buber, *The Way of Man* (New York: Citadel Press, 2002; originally delivered as a lecture in 1947).

a glimpse into another world. A bold, booming city rising out of the desert – like ambition built it brick by brick. Everything about it lit something up in me. The futuristic skyline, the energy, the sense that anything was possible. It stirred something deep. This place didn't just look like a dream – it felt like a mirror to my own aspirations.

One afternoon during the trip, Dad casually mentioned the idea of me coming to live with him in the UAE.

At the time, it felt like a distant possibility. But it stayed with me.

A few years later, with my teenage years spiralling, that opportunity rose again – this time through my grandad, trying to steer me before I drifted too far.

'I'm worried about you, son,' he said one day, eyes full of concern. 'Things can't go on like this. You need to break the cycle.'

He'd seen the mess I was getting into. And in that moment, I could see he cared.

'Have you thought about getting away?' he asked. 'Maybe go stay with your dad in Dubai for a bit?'

I wasn't sure. I'd never lived anywhere but the Borders. Dubai felt worlds apart from the misty hills and familiar streets I'd grown up with. But the idea of something new – something more – had always tugged at me. And now it was calling louder than ever.

'Dad,' I said one night on the phone, hesitantly.

'Aye?' came the familiar Glaswegian accent.

'I wanted to ask . . . do you remember that holiday in Dubai, when you said I could come live with you?'

'Aye,' he replied.

'I was wondering . . . maybe I could come out now?'

There was a pause.

Then, 'Aye, why no?'

He went on, 'You'll need to get a welding qualification – I'll get you a job through the family out here.'

And that was it. Something clicked in me. I got the qualification in no time and was soon on a flight back to the Emirates. I was proud of how quickly I made it happen. When I put my mind to something, I could do it. I could change things.

This was the start of something new. A clean slate. A life that could've gone a very different way.

Or so I thought.

***

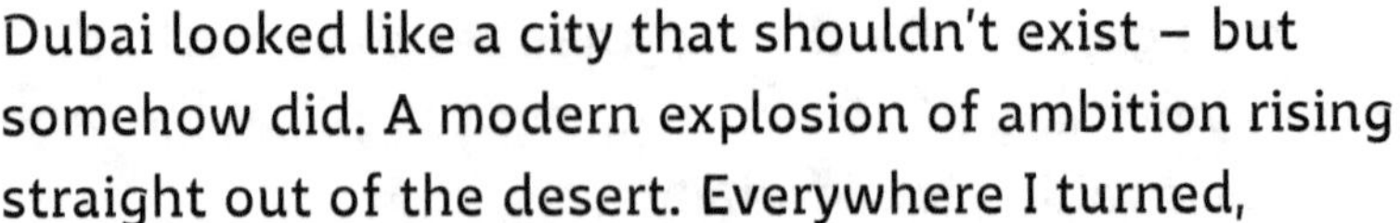

Dubai looked like a city that shouldn't exist – but somehow did. A modern explosion of ambition rising straight out of the desert. Everywhere I turned, something was being built, expanded, imagined into being. Glass towers stretched into the sky as if pointing to the future. It was bold, fast-moving, alive. It felt like anything could happen here.

And I was buzzing to be part of it.

The first three months flew by. I loved the pace of life – the warmth, the beaches, the people. I even had to fly out to Qatar to renew my visa, a requirement for staying on. It all felt exciting. Like I was stepping into the life I'd always wanted.

The beaches were stunning – white sand, clear water, teeming with tropical fish. I'd swim to cool off from the heat, always staying close to shore. There were stories about sharks getting through the protective nets, even attacking people. It was rare, but real enough to keep you in the shallows.

Looking back, that's how it was with me too.

From the outside, I looked like I was cruising – young, working, living in one of the most glamorous cities in the world. I had my foot on the gas, overtaking the past, flying down the highway of life. But somewhere inside, I was still stuck in the shallows. Still restless. Still searching.

The truth was, I missed home.

I missed the banter, the boys, the buzz of parties, and the pull of everything I'd left behind. And slowly, quietly, that ache started to grow.

***

We hadn't officially broken up when I moved to Dubai. Maybe we should have – but we didn't. I stayed in touch with my girlfriend back home. The calls weren't frequent, but they were enough to keep something alive.

Then came this one.

'Hey,' I said, trying to sound upbeat as the call connected.

'Ricky?' Her voice was half-lost in the background noise – music blaring, people laughing, the familiar sound of a party in full swing.

'Aye, it's me.'

'Hold on – let me speak!' someone shouted in the background.

Then another voice cut in – *'Bro! We all miss you, man! When you coming back? It's just no the same without you!'*

More voices joined the chorus. *'Tell him to get back!'*

'It's Ricky! Shhh!'

Even through the distortion of the call, I could hear the buzz. The closeness. The madness. And I felt the ache of not being there. They sounded like they were having the time of their lives . . . without me.

Conversations like that didn't make it easier – they made it worse. I missed the banter, the mess, the sense of belonging. I missed feeling like part of something, even if that something was a disaster in the making.

The longer I stayed in Dubai, the louder that ache became. What had started as a dream opportunity began to feel like a cage. I was lonely. Out of sync. Surrounded by sand and success, but craving the familiar chaos I'd grown up with.

Eventually, I made a decision.

I didn't fly to Qatar to renew my visa a second time. I booked a flight home instead.

To this day, I wonder what might have been if I'd stayed. If I'd pushed through. If I'd seen it through to something better. I'm sure my dad was disappointed – I know I was.

That would be the only time we ever lived together. But it gave us shared memories. And even now, if he's had a few whiskies, he'll laugh and tell stories from those Dubai days. I'm grateful for that.

But, deep down, I know this was my first major fork in the road.

And I took the wrong turn.

Looking back, it's clear – this was my first big turning point. A real chance to rewrite my story. But I wasn't ready. I still didn't know how to live without the buzz, without the chaos. The loneliness exposed something in me I didn't yet understand. Instead of facing it, I ran from it – back to what was familiar, even if it was destructive.

And in doing so, I let opportunity slip through my fingers.

***

Colin was – and still is – a character in the truest sense of the word. A natural wheeler-dealer, with a streak of entrepreneurial flair that could have taken him far in life . . . if it hadn't been rooted so deeply in the drug scene.

He wasn't just a mate, he was like a brother. In a life full of chaos, Colin was oddly reliable – when it came to scoring drugs, he rarely let you down. Unlike most users, he always had something on him. And if he didn't, he knew exactly where to get it. Valium, tranquillisers – you name it, he could sort it.

Valium had a grip on me I couldn't fully admit at the time. It wasn't just about dulling pain or numbing guilt. I loved the feeling it gave me – calm, confident, in control. Like the version of myself I thought I was supposed to be. It didn't feel like a crutch. It felt like a key. And once I'd tasted that feeling, I couldn't imagine life without it.

So when I landed back in Hawick and Colin and I got a construction labouring job in Edinburgh, it felt like a small lifeline. We were working on a new wing at the Western General Hospital – early mornings, commuting from Hawick, hard graft, decent pay. For a while, it gave me a bit of rhythm. Something steady.

One day, we noticed the college next door – Telford College. Restless as ever, we wandered in and ended up enrolling on an IT course starting that August. The plan was to commute from Hawick until we could move closer. As expected, Colin dipped out not long after. But I stuck it out.

Through a mate at college, I found a flat not far from campus. The area had a reputation – rough, with a colourful history – but the neighbours were sound. I didn't mind it. It wasn't glamorous, but it was mine. A base. A new beginning.

For a little while, it felt like things were moving forward.

But just as I started to find my feet again, the past caught up with me in the shape of someone I thought I'd left behind.

***

It was New Year's Eve, 1999. Everyone was buzzing about the new millennium, the world on edge with Y2K panic and midnight countdowns. But for me, the real surprise came in the form of an old face.

Liam.

We crossed paths at a party to see in the year 2000. He'd been living down in Newcastle, but as soon as I saw him, it felt like no time had passed. Same sly grin. Same magnetic energy.

It wasn't long before we were reminiscing, catching up, talking plans. We both wanted a fresh start. New year, new millennium, new city. So, by January, we moved into my flat together.

At least on paper, it looked like things were moving in the right direction.

I was in full-time education at college. We had our own place. I was technically building towards something. But underneath it all, nothing had changed. I was still drinking almost daily. Smoking weed like it was second nature. Taking anything we could get our hands on to keep the buzz going.

Colin was still about too, dropping by regularly with a steady supply of Valium, tranquillisers, and whatever else was going round at the time.

Petty crime was just part of the lifestyle – easy, familiar, justifiable when you're already blurring the lines.

We thought we were living. But we were blind to the fact we were already teetering on the edge of something darker.

What started out as a hopeful escape had become a mask. A fresh coat of paint over a house that was already falling apart inside.

***

Our flat was on the ground floor, with a small garden that opened straight onto the street. From the path, you could see right through the living room window. But that didn't bother us. We kept to ourselves, and even though the area had a rough reputation, the neighbours were decent. We didn't feel unsafe.

That all changed one night.

Colin was up visiting and happened to answer the door when two guys from the area showed up, saying they were looking to buy. I was in the other room when I heard them come in. Something about their tone made my ears prick up – too casual, too confident, like they knew exactly what they were walking into.

They came through the hallway slow and cautious – one stocky, the other wiry – eyes twitching, scanning the room. There was an edge in the air I couldn't quite place, but I knew I didn't like it.

'So, what have you got then?' the heavier one asked, sharp and demanding.

'What are you after?' Colin replied, cool but alert.

Silence.

Then Colin said, 'I've got some pills . . .'

A loud thud, followed by a yell – 'Argh! What the– !'

I ran in and saw Colin shoved over the couch, pinned by the big guy while the other started rifling through drawers, shouting at him.

'Where is it?! Grab it!'

They weren't customers – they were here to take.

Adrenaline surged. I grabbed the nearest thing I could find – a pint glass – and charged.

'You snakes!' I roared, slamming it into the side of the heavy one's face. It shattered on impact, spraying blood across the wall.

Colin scrambled up like he'd been lit on fire. He snatched the iron from beside the TV and swung it with full force, connecting with the wiry guy's head. A sickening crack, plastic flying, blood splashing across the wooden floor.

They both bolted – stumbling, shouting, bleeding – all thoughts of robbery gone as fast as they came.

We stood frozen, gasping for breath. The room was wrecked – glass on the floor, blood on the walls, the air thick with sweat and shock.

'Ricky – your hand, mate. Look!'

I looked down and saw blood pouring from my palm, dripping between my fingers. The glass had sliced clean through the tendons. I couldn't move two fingers at all.

'I need to get to hospital,' I said, my voice flat with shock.

Colin and Liam came with me. We made it to A&E, and I was rushed in for surgery. It would take time to heal – stitches, nerve repair, physio – but the physical wound wasn't the only thing that needed fixing.

Until that night, we'd felt relatively settled. We weren't looking over our shoulders. But after what happened, everything changed. The sense of safety we'd built, even in a messy lifestyle, was shattered.

The flat didn't feel like home anymore. It felt like a target.

And we knew we couldn't stay.

***

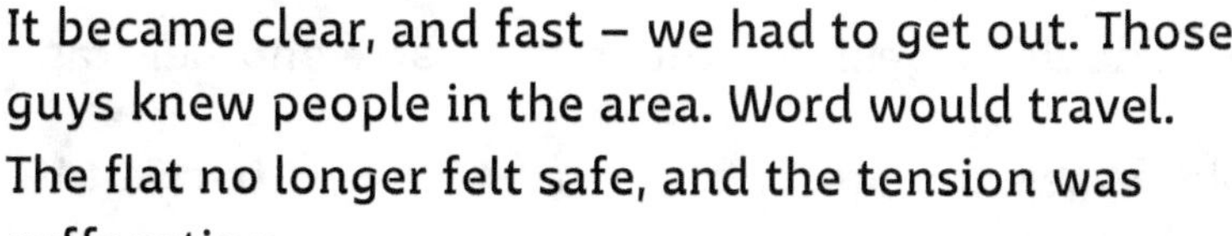

It became clear, and fast – we had to get out. Those guys knew people in the area. Word would travel. The flat no longer felt safe, and the tension was suffocating.

But strangely, as we packed up and planned our next move, something unexpected happened.

Despite everything – the drinking, the drugs, the violence – I'd managed to finish my HND. I don't know how I scraped through, but I did. Even I was shocked. For all my self-sabotage, my determination still flickered beneath the chaos. It was fragile, but it hadn't gone out completely.

That qualification gave me the chance to enter directly into the third year of university – something I'd never dreamed of. Never even considered possible.

And just like that, I was accepted.

We moved across the city into a new flat near the university campus. It felt like a fresh start. Another chance.

But the chaos hadn't left me.

My substance use was still full-blown. I scraped through classes by the skin of my teeth. Anxiety and shame were always lurking. To cope, I went to my GP and walked away with a prescription – diazepam, nitrazepam, antidepressants, and opiate-based painkillers.

What should've been a safety net became another trap.

I told myself the prescription was just a crutch. But it quickly became a chain.

Beneath the surface, I was crumbling. The closer I got to finishing something, the more that voice in my head came back:

You'll never make it in IT or multimedia.
You're not good enough.
They'll see through you. You're a fraud.

And so, to silence it, I kept reaching for the only thing that worked.

***

'Right, lads, now that Ricky's got his degree, where do we go next?' Liam asked, that familiar glint of excitement in his eyes.

'What about somewhere in England?' Colin offered, always up for a new idea.

'Sheffield,' Liam nodded. 'I've been a couple of times – good feel to it.'

I felt something stir at the thought. Maybe this was it – a new start, away from the chaos. I didn't say much, but the idea lingered.

Colin looked over at us. 'Here, why don't you both move in with me for a bit? Save some money, get things sorted, then make the move.'

I hesitated. 'Aye, alright – but just for a wee while. I'm no wantin' to get stuck in the Borders again. There's not exactly much goin' on there, is there?'

'Naw, there's no!' Liam laughed. 'Right then – move in, save up, and then it's Sheffield!'

We all burst out laughing, caught in the buzz of the moment.

That was the plan.

But Sheffield never happened.

Once I finished my course, we moved out of the city and in with Colin at his place in the Borders, thinking it would only be temporary.

But what was meant to be short-term became permanent. Living with Colin was too easy – a roof over my head, no rent stress, and more importantly . . . an endless supply of what I needed. Unlike most users, Colin always had something on him.

I knew he was on methadone, but I hadn't realised he was selling heroin. That changed fast.

At first, I stuck to my usual mix – alcohol, diazepam, the comfort I knew. But it wasn't long before heroin entered the picture. Slowly, it started replacing the drink. The switch wasn't planned. It just happened. A wee line here, a smoke there. And soon enough, I was in deeper than ever before.

Diazepam, though – that stayed central. Always. I loved them. And now, heroin had joined the mix and begun to tighten its grip – a grip like nothing else I had ever experienced.

The new chapter I thought I was stepping into . . . was already slipping through my fingers.

And what came next would drag me further than I ever thought I'd go.

Chapter 3

Into the Depths

Bang! Bang! Bang!

'It's the police! Stay where you are and keep your hands where we can see them!' The leading officer's voice thundered through the flat as five or six officers stormed in, their boots slamming against the wooden floor.

My eyes snapped open, dragging me from a drug-induced stupor. The harsh glare of torches sliced through the darkness. Panic surged through my veins as I tried to process the chaos unfolding around me.

'Where are the drugs?' an officer barked, his eyes drilling into me.

Crap. My mind raced. Where were they? I glanced at Liam, who sat frozen, his expression unreadable.

'What you on about?' Liam shot back, defiant.

'Don't play dumb,' another officer snapped. 'We know they're here. Don't make this harder than it needs to be.'

Drawers yanked open. Furniture overturned. Our flat was being dismantled piece by piece. My heart pounded as I desperately tried to remember where the stash might be. I knew the second they found anything, we were done.

'Sarge, don't worry,' one officer chuckled. 'Even if they don't talk, we've got enough here to send them down.' He held up a small bag of heroin, some tablets, and the tell-tale set of scales.

A pit opened in my stomach.

'You're going down, you scumbags,' the officer sneered as he yanked my arms behind my back and clicked the handcuffs into place. A jolt of pain shot through my shoulder.

'Watch what you're doing! You're twisting my arm!' Liam snapped as they shoved us out the door, down the narrow stairwell, and into the waiting police van. The night air bit at my skin, but it was nothing compared to the dread curling in my gut.

Inside the van, I exhaled shakily. 'Is there any more in the house?' I muttered.

Liam hesitated, then shook his head. 'Not that I know of. Colin's probably got it stashed somewhere outside.'

Relief flickered for a moment – then vanished.

After a long silence, Liam turned to me, jaw tight. 'By the sounds of things, bro, we're getting remanded. They found enough to send us down – especially the scales.'

I let out a long breath, fists clenched. 'I know.'

Liam shrugged, trying to play it off. 'Oh well. Here we go again.'

For him, it was routine. For me, this was a first. I stared out the van's tiny window, watching the town blur past, knowing that by Monday morning, we'd be standing in court.

And as expected, we were remanded in custody at HMP Edinburgh – our fate sealed with the slam of a judge's gavel.

***

'Addiction is the parasite of the soul,' said one of the lads, leaning back on his bunk.

'What are you on about now?' someone asked, unimpressed.

'I was reading something mad. Some parasites feed off their host while it's still alive. They've got these horrible wee tools – suckers, claws, hooks – designed to cling on and drain the life out bit by bit.'

'You what, mate?'

'Seriously. They keep the host just alive enough to survive, but never enough to thrive. It's not in the parasite's interest to kill its meal ticket.'

Another inmate snorted. 'You're a smart one, you are!'

Someone else laughed, picking up the joke. 'Here, "Smarty Marty"!'

I couldn't help but smirk. It was classic jailhouse banter – part humour, part deflection.

But the first guy wasn't backing down. 'Tell me that's not like addiction. We do things we swore we never would – to feed that thing inside us. We drain our families, lie to everyone, cheat the people we love. All to keep the parasite satisfied.'

'Nah, I don't agree,' said another, shifting tone. 'We're worse. I was worse. At least parasites act on instinct. I knew what I was doing and still did it.'

There was a pause.

'Cheer up,' the first guy said with a laugh. 'You've not gone as far as altering your victims' DNA so predators are drawn to them – just so you can be eaten and go infect something else in the process!'

The room burst out laughing again.

'Not yet anyway,' someone joked. 'Sounds like something my dealer would try!'

There's a kind of dark humour that grows inside prison – a shield we use to survive. Everyone finds their own way to cope.

***

Sitting on remand in HMP Edinburgh, I stared up at the cracked ceiling, wondering how my life had come to this. The weight of it pressed down like a slab of concrete. I was grateful to be sharing a cell with Liam – that small mercy mattered more than most realise. You never knew who you might get locked in with.

One lad we knew from Hawick wasn't so lucky. He'd ended up sharing with a guy who gave him the creeps. One night, he woke to find his cellmate standing over him – staring. Eyes dark, unmoving. A scuffle broke out, and half the hall was jolted awake by the noise.

The next morning, the lad came into the communal area with a busted lip and a black eye.

'He looked as bad as me!' he said bitterly, rubbing his jaw. 'I woke up, saw the guy looming over me, so I smacked him! I'd heard rumours, but still – that was a shock!'

He didn't finish the sentence. We were already howling with laughter.

Shaking his head, he muttered, 'At least he won't try that again.'

'Well, my new cellmate's sound, anyway,' he added, still chuckling.

We may have laughed, but underneath the jokes was real unease. It made me all the more grateful to be with someone I knew.

The prescription meds dulled the withdrawal symptoms, but they didn't kill the cravings. Heroin, diazepam – we talked about them constantly. About the high, the escape, the silence they brought. The hunger never left. It stalked us in every quiet moment.

***

Two weeks in, we were falling into the rhythm of prison life when something unexpected happened.

One afternoon, as we got ready for recreation, there was a knock at the door. A voice followed – one we recognised immediately.

'Awrite, boys! How yous doin'?'

In strolled Colin, grinning like he'd just won the lottery.

'Got myself lifted on purpose,' he said, puffed up with pride. 'Made sure it was serious enough to get remanded so I could land in with you two – and bring a surprise.'

Without missing a beat, he walked straight to the tiny toilet cubicle.

'Someone keep a lookout for the screws,' he muttered, pulling the door shut behind him.

Liam and I exchanged a look – part disbelief, part anticipation. We could hear faint rustling, the clink of something hitting the floor. We both stared at the gap under the door, holding our breath.

A few moments later, Colin emerged, holding a small bundle: tablets, a bit of hash, and – most importantly – a little heroin.

'Here you go, lads. Sorry about what happened at mine. Thanks for not grassing.'

Relief washed over us. For a moment, the tension lifted. We could finally escape – just for a while.

But we had to be careful. If word got out, we'd be surrounded in minutes. Everyone in that place was desperate for a hit. And we weren't in the mood for sharing.

This was for us.

The remand lasted a couple of months, and by then, my mind was already set on the next move.

I decided to move in with my girlfriend back in Hawick – a different relationship from before. Part of me dreaded returning to the town, but another part craved the illusion of stability. A fresh start, I told myself. Maybe this time, things would be different.

But addiction has a way of poisoning even the best intentions.

It lasted a year. A year of fleeting highs and creeping lows, of love and disappointment, of pretending I had it together when I was barely keeping myself afloat. When the relationship finally ended, I got my own flat in the town centre – and with it came full-blown isolation and chaos.

For months, I scraped by, just managing to keep my addiction fed. The routine was suffocating: waking up, chasing a fix, making sure I had enough to get through the day, then doing it all again. Every single day, just enough to avoid facing the dreaded withdrawal.

Until one morning, as I sat in my freezing flat, the thought hit me like a punch to the gut.

What's the point of this? Scraping by, barely living, constantly on edge. *What if I just sold the stuff myself?*

Colin had made a fortune doing it. I knew how the game worked, and I had the contacts. Heroin and street Valium – my two poisons of choice – were always in demand.

Before long, I wasn't just using. I was dealing.

And addiction, which had already buried its claws into me, dragged me down even further.

'Ricky, open the door mate!'

The voice jolted me awake. A loud bang rattled my front door. I squinted at my alarm clock. *Seriously? It's only 6 a.m.*

I groaned, pulled the covers over my head, and tried to ignore him.

Rattle, rattle. The letterbox flapped open. 'Ricky, mate! Open the door!'

Desperation dripped from his voice. I didn't need to ask why he was here. He was rattling – clearly looking to secure his fix at any cost. Probably hadn't slept, probably sweating buckets, his body screaming for a hit.

I clenched my jaw. I wasn't in the mood for this.

'Ricky, please! I've got cash, man!'

My patience snapped. Annoyed – but more worried about him waking the neighbours – I stayed silent. Eventually, after a few long seconds, I heard his footsteps retreat down the stairwell.

Blowing out a sigh of relief, I lay there for a moment, staring at the ceiling. But I was wide awake now, and my body was starting to scream its own demands.

Right. I need a fix myself.

Dragging myself out of bed, I scurried to the toilet, bracing against the freezing air. The flat was like an icebox – ancient storage heaters that cost a fortune to run meant I relied on a tiny blower heater to keep whatever room I was in bearable.

I flicked the kettle on. The heat from the coffee would do more than warm me up – it would speed up the tablets I'd just thrown down my throat, helping them hit faster.

Coffee in one hand, lighter in the other, I sat on the edge of my bed, tinfoil at the ready. The ritual was second nature by now.

The lighter flicked. The heroin melted. The smoke curled.

I inhaled deeply, closing my eyes as the familiar warmth washed over me. The craving dulled. My mind stilled. For a few fleeting moments, I felt . . . normal.

But normal was a lie. Because as soon as the high began to fade, the gnawing emptiness returned.

My mental health was in free fall. Depression and anxiety clung to me like shadows, creeping in every time the drugs wore off. The panic attacks had become routine – if I didn't have enough diazepam in my system, my body went into overdrive, my heart racing, my breath shortening, my hands trembling.

At times, I feared the withdrawals from the diazepam more than the heroin. If I ran low, I'd be sent into a desperate frenzy, scouring every contact I had to make sure I never ran out.

I was trapped in an endless cycle. Chasing, using, dreading the thought of withdrawal.

I didn't know how to escape. I didn't know if I even wanted to.

I was stuck. And I was sinking fast.

***

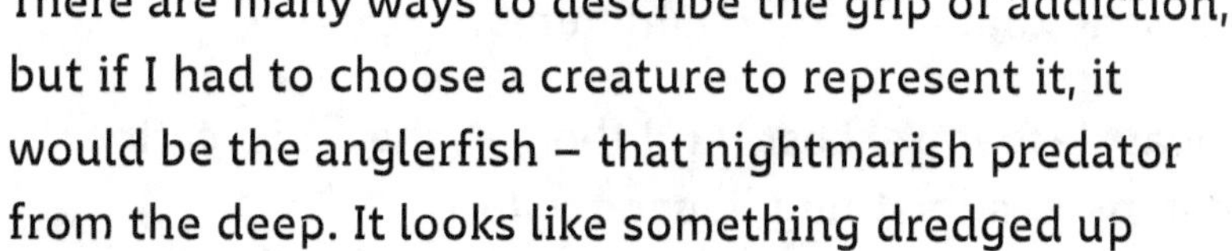

There are many ways to describe the grip of addiction, but if I had to choose a creature to represent it, it would be the anglerfish – that nightmarish predator from the deep. It looks like something dredged up from a bad dream, a relic from the Cretaceous period that still haunts the darkest depths of the ocean.

The anglerfish lurks in places we've barely explored, its strange light luring prey towards it through complete blackness. It offers the illusion of hope – a glimmer in the dark – only to consume whatever draws near.

That's what addiction does. It dangles the promise of relief, of escape, of something better . . . but it's a lie. The light isn't the end of the tunnel. It's another trap. Another snare.

***

It was at my lowest – when the darkness felt endless – that something began to shift. I never cried out to God. Never whispered a prayer. But now, looking back, I believe he saw beyond the bravado I'd carefully built.

On the surface, I seemed to be doing fine – money in my pocket, drugs in my system, a car to drive, a girlfriend at my side. To the outside world, I looked like I was surviving, maybe even thriving.

But inside? I was crumbling.

Every high was followed by a deeper low. Every escape left me more trapped. The emptiness gnawed at me – an ache that no drug could numb.

I was desperate. Lost. And then, in that suffocating darkness, something began to shift.

Not in my thinking – I wasn't searching for God. He wasn't on my mind. I wasn't praying, or hoping, or even looking for help.

But now, looking back, I believe he was already there. I believe he saw the cry beneath the chaos – the silent ache of a soul too numb to speak.

And in that place of despair, a flicker of light began to shine.

Faint at first. Almost imperceptible.

But real.

A pull. A whisper. A quiet sense that maybe – just maybe – I wasn't beyond saving.

Chapter 4

Seeds of Faith

Knock! Knock! Knock!

'Ricky, it's me – open the door, mate.'

The summer sun spilled through the thin curtains, casting long streaks of light across the cluttered living room. One of the lads, slouched on the couch, exhaled a thin stream of smoke before setting his foil down.

'I'll get it,' he muttered, dragging himself up and shuffling towards the front door.

The moment the living room door swung open, one of the lads stepped inside, bringing someone new with him. I didn't recognise the guy – big build, short hair, the kind of face that'd clearly been around the block a few times. The lad on the couch clocked my hesitation and quickly jumped in.

'He's looking for a bag. That's his mate, Nathan – I've met him before. He's awright.'

I shifted my gaze towards the doorway, locking eyes with the first lad, then sizing up Nathan. Before I could speak, Nathan filled the silence.

'Awright, mate,' he said, his thick Glaswegian accent giving him away.

'Awright,' I replied, keeping my tone neutral as I turned back to chasing the dragon. 'Sort them out.'

The deal was quick – just another exchange, another face in the revolving door of that life.

What I didn't know then was that this seemingly insignificant moment – this passing introduction – was about to play a far bigger role in my story than I ever could have imagined. As if it had all been orchestrated for a purpose I couldn't yet see . . .

'Who was that you were talking to?' I asked, raising an eyebrow as Nathan hung up the phone.

'Ah, just my support worker from rehab,' he replied, a little too casually – his tone laced with something between guilt and amusement.

'Rehab?' I echoed, frowning in surprise.

'Aye. I moved to Hawick for college after finishing a programme in Duns.'

'Duns? I never even knew there was a rehab in Duns!'

'Aye,' he nodded, shifting in his seat. 'After you finish the programme, you go into what they call phase four – it's the final part, where you reintegrate into the community after spending ten to twelve months in rehab.'

'Ten to twelve months?' I whistled. 'That sounds more like a jail sentence than rehab!'

We both burst out laughing, but as the chuckles faded, Nathan's expression changed.

'Aye, you're no far wrong there, mate,' he smirked – then his face turned more serious. 'But . . . it doesnae half transform your life.'

I paused, studying him. 'What do you mean by that?'

'Aw, nothin', mate,' he muttered, shaking his head with an undertone of sadness. 'I mean . . . it clearly didnae work, did it?' He held out his tinfoil, let out a short laugh, and proceeded to smoke his heroin.

Something in the way he said it lingered – heavier than the smoke curling between us. I hadn't known he'd been through rehab, let alone that he was now stringing along some poor support worker, pretending to stay clean. This wasn't just a slip – it was a full-blown relapse. He'd done the time, completed the course . . . and now he was back here, using again.

But strangely, that moment marked the beginning of something.

Amongst all the people I knew in addiction, there was something different about Nathan. As our friendship grew, he opened up about his past – growing up in one of Glasgow's roughest estates, running with gangs, guns, prison sentences, chaos. I listened, trying to reconcile his words with the guy sitting in front of me.

But you seem like such a decent guy, I thought. *How could you have been involved in all that?*

And yet, despite the relapse, despite the mess, there was something in what he said – about his life transforming, about things being different – that wouldn't leave my mind.

I didn't realise it then, but God was about to use this unlikely friendship – and these broken moments – to begin a transformation my soul had been longing for.

***

'What on earth is this you're listening to, Nathan?'

'Matt Redman,' he said, grinning. 'D'you like it?'

'Aye, it's no bad. But who even is Matt Redman? Never heard of him!'

'It's Christian music.'

'Christian?' I said, frowning. 'I thought that was just hymns and auld folk singing in church!'

Nathan burst out laughing. 'Nah, mate! There's some class Christian stuff out there. It's aw I listen to now.'

I gave him a look. 'Why Christian, though?'

''Cause I'm a Christian,' he said, still smiling.

I blinked. 'Wait, what? Since when?'

'Mind I told you about that rehab I was in?'

'Aye.'

'It was a Christian rehab,' he said, his voice a bit softer now. 'That's what I meant when I said it doesnae half transform your life – becoming a Christian, I mean.'

I frowned. 'What d'you mean by that? Becoming a Christian? What does that even mean?'

Nathan leaned forward a bit. 'It means believing Jesus is the Son of God. That he died for our sins and rose again. And if we ask him to forgive us, and decide to follow him, he gives us a fresh start. No just a clean slate – but a new heart. Something changes on the inside.'

I looked at him, half-confused. 'What are you on about?'

He chuckled and picked up a book from the windowsill. 'Here – was gonna offer you this earlier.' He held out a Bible.

I leaned back. 'Nah, you're alright. That's no for me. I won't read it.'

He didn't push. Just looked at me and asked, 'What d'you think aboot God?'

I shrugged. 'I dunno. I believe in something, but no idea what it is.'

'Fair enough,' he nodded.

I paused. 'You ever seen that film, *Constantine*?'

'Aye,' he said, raising an eyebrow.

'Made me think a bit. All that stuff – angels, demons, battles we can't see. Do you reckon it's real?'

He tilted his head. 'Maybe. But films are made to entertain, eh? Doesn't mean it's all true.'

'Still makes you wonder,' I said, my voice trailing.

Then he said, 'Ever thought aboot rehab, Ricky?'

I laughed and shook my head. 'Naw, mate, I'm no interested in that.'

Looking for a way out of the conversation, I waved my hand. 'Anyway, let's get back to business. Pass me the tinfoil over . . .'

***

Walking home that dark evening after leaving Nathan's, my mind was a whirlwind of thoughts. The conversation we'd just had – it was like stepping into another world, one I never expected to be part of.

Nathan – a Christian? That threw me. I'd known him for a while now, but I had no idea. And that music . . . Matt Redman? Christian rehab?

I shook my head, trying to brush off the unease creeping in. *Na, man, I'm sorted.* I've got my own house, a girlfriend, all the drugs I need, and plenty of cash.

I didn't need rehab. Especially not Christian rehab.

But as much as I tried to push it away, the thoughts about God clung to me – stubborn and relentless. Could there really be a God?

I exhaled sharply, stuffing my hands into my pockets as I walked, my breath visible in the cold night air.

Why is this bothering me so much?

And then, like a film reel playing in my mind, I was taken back – to another night, ten years previous, another dark street, another version of myself walking home alone . . . wrestling with the same question.

***

Taking the brownish-green lump of compacted cannabis resin, I began to crumble it between my fingers – back then, that was how everyone rolled their joints. It was just another weekend at a mate's house, laughter filling the air, the room thick with smoke and the familiar clinking of beer bottles.

'Where are the skins?' I asked, trying to busy myself with rolling, hoping to avoid what I knew was coming – the dreaded beer run.

The run itself wasn't the issue. The problem was who I had to pass to get to the fridge. Sitting in the living room was my mate's mum, who I knew was a committed Christian. Not just someone who went to church on Sundays, but someone who genuinely lived by their faith – following Jesus' teachings in everyday life. The thought of facing that kind of presence while I reeked of alcohol and smoke made my stomach twist.

'I'll roll it,' I offered quickly.

'Nah, not happening,' one of the lads smirked, clocking my plan straight away. 'It's your turn to get the beers.'

'I'll roll the joint – you go,' I tried again, glancing at another for backup.

'Nope,' came the reply, already reaching for the papers.

'Come on – beer run?' I asked the last of them, my voice now edging into desperation.

He shook his head. 'Nice try, mate. It's your turn.'

I sighed heavily. There was no getting out of it.

Making my way through the living room as quietly as possible, I stepped into the kitchen, determined to grab the beers and get back before any awkward conversation could unfold.

But the silence hit me first. No TV. No radio. Just stillness.

It was unsettling. Who chooses to sit in silence on a Saturday night? And in the living room, of all places?

I'd been noticed. Great.

'Erm . . . hi,' I muttered, shifting uncomfortably.

The woman I'd been hoping to avoid looked up at me. Her expression was calm, kind. Inviting.

'Come here, Ricky. Take a seat.'

I hesitated, but something in her demeanour made it impossible to refuse.

I don't remember much of what she said, but I remember how she made me feel. There was something different about her – her gentleness, her warmth, the complete lack of judgement in her voice. There was no 'you shouldn't be doing this' or 'sort your life out'. Just kindness. Compassion.

'Can I say a wee prayer for you, Ricky?'

I nodded without thinking.

As she prayed, something unexpected happened – tears welled up in my eyes and spilled down my cheeks. I wasn't sad. I wasn't ashamed. It felt . . . comforting. Like a release I didn't even know I needed.

Before I left, she handed me a small, folded leaflet – a tract – with some words about faith and the need for God.

In the bathroom, I made sure there was no trace of tears on my face before walking back into the haze of laughter and smoke. I felt different. Not convicted. Not guilty. Just . . . lighter.

Later that night, as I walked home, my fingers brushed against the paper in my pocket. Pulling it out, I read the words under the streetlight. It spoke about how we were made for relationship with God, how Jesus came to rescue us, and how, when we choose to believe in him and ask for forgiveness, he sends the Holy Spirit to live in us – to give us the power to live a new life.

What if this is true? What if there's more to life than I ever thought? What if . . . there's a God?

The next morning, I found the tract still in my pocket. I stared at it for a moment. Then, shaking my head, I crumpled it up and threw it in the bin.

No chance.

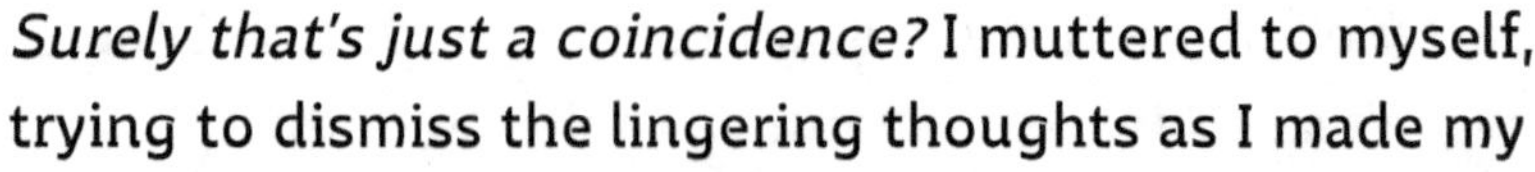

Surely that's just a coincidence? I muttered to myself, trying to dismiss the lingering thoughts as I made my way home from Nathan's house. But no matter how hard I tried to shake it, these 'Christian connections' unsettled me.

The further I walked, the deeper my mind wandered. What connection did I even have to God? My thoughts drifted back to my childhood – Granny taking me to the odd church service, the occasional school assembly where we'd sing hymns without really thinking about the words. But that was it. Nothing deep. Nothing meaningful.

Well, apart from football, of course.

In Scotland, religion wasn't just about churches and prayers – it was tangled up in the fabric of everyday life, woven into the chants of football stadiums and the rivalries that ran deeper than the sport itself. The old divide: Catholic vs Protestant. Rangers vs Celtic.

My dad's family were Catholic, though none of them really practised. My mum's side were Protestant, but again, church wasn't something we did. It was more a label, something we were born into rather than believed in. As a child, I'd been christened a Protestant, but it didn't mean much to me. Just another formality.

Then there was my mum's boyfriend at the time – the father of my youngest brother. When I was about eleven, he moved in with us. A staunch Rangers man, he was deep into the Orange Lodge – a Protestant group known for its parades and strong links to

Rangers and unionist culture. My dad wasn't pleased, to say the least.

Soon, I was being taken to Ibrox, swept up in the energy of the stands, the sea of blue, the chants that rang through the stadium. At the time, it all felt normal – just part of life, just part of being a Rangers fan.

But now, as I walked the empty streets, Nathan's words still echoing in my mind, I was starting to see things differently.

Maybe religion wasn't just about football. Maybe there was more. So much more.

***

In the months that followed, rehab became a persistent whisper in my mind. No matter how hard I tried to ignore it, the thought of breaking free from heroin – and the darkness of depression – kept creeping back. Could I actually do it? Could I really be free?

But then came the fear: diazepam.

If heroin had trapped my body, diazepam had wrapped itself around my mind. I loved them. Needed them. The thought of living without that hazy cushion, that numbing safety net, was unbearable. Every time I considered rehab, the same thought tormented me: *How could I cope without them?*

Still, the idea wouldn't go away.

So I started researching the rehab Nathan had been to – Teen Challenge.[6] The more I read, the more a plan began to form in my mind. A master plan, or so I thought.

In November 2006, I finally decided to apply. But not to the centre in the Scottish Borders – too close to home. Instead, I set my sights on Wales. A fresh start. A clean slate.

But my thinking was still warped.

I told myself I'd go for three months, just long enough to get off heroin. Then I'd relocate to Swansea, sign up at a new doctor's surgery, and get back on my diazepam prescription. Because no matter how much I wanted freedom, I couldn't imagine life without them.

At least, not yet.

***

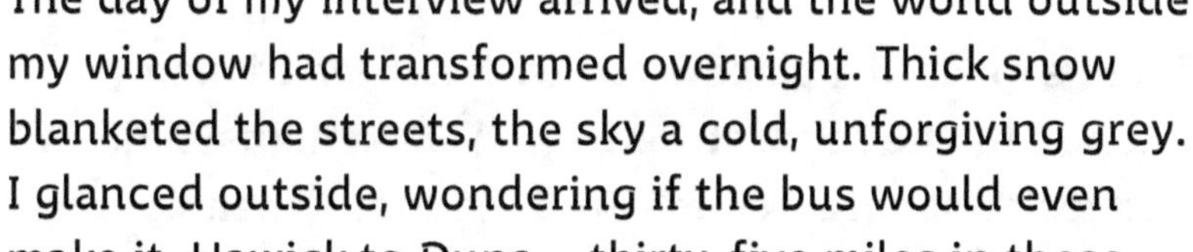

The day of my interview arrived, and the world outside my window had transformed overnight. Thick snow blanketed the streets, the sky a cold, unforgiving grey. I glanced outside, wondering if the bus would even make it. Hawick to Duns – thirty-five miles in these conditions? It felt impossible.

But the bus came. Through the white wilderness, we moved forward.

6. Teen Challenge UK – Official website: *About Us* https://www.teenchallenge.org.uk/about-us (accessed August 2025).

Upon arriving in Duns, a worker from the rehab met me and drove me the rest of the way. As we ventured deeper into the countryside, I felt a growing unease. It was like stepping into another world – remote, untouched, eerily silent. The road twisted through snow-draped hills, towering trees standing like frozen sentinels. It felt like Narnia. I half expected to see a lamp post flickering through the frost or Aslan himself stepping from behind the trees.

The rehab centre sat at the top of a hill, its old stone walls looming over the vast white expanse below. The stark, leafless trees surrounding the property only intensified the sense of isolation. It felt like a place forgotten by time. A shiver ran down my spine – was I stepping into my salvation, or my exile?

Yet, the moment I stepped inside, everything changed.

Warmth. Laughter. A world away from the cold silence outside.

I had expected a place filled with hardened men, shaped by the same streets I had walked. Instead, the residents greeted me with kindness, their eyes reflecting something I couldn't quite place – *peace? freedom? hope?*

I wasn't sure what unnerved me more – the eerie silence of the landscape or the warmth of the welcome.

The interview went well. I was accepted.

A flood of mixed emotions washed over me: excitement, fear, a gnawing uncertainty. The thought of coming off the drugs and medication after so many years? Terrifying.

During the waiting period, I had to call the rehab centre every week to prove my commitment. Each call felt like stepping closer to the edge of a cliff. Two months dragged by, each day heavy with anticipation.

Then, the date came – 28th March 2007.

Up to this point, I had told almost no one. Only my family knew, and I had sworn them to secrecy. I quietly began the process of giving up my flat, tying up loose ends, preparing for the unknown.

I had no idea how life-changing this decision would be.

Chapter 5

Shock to the System

'Hurry up, Ricky! We don't want to miss the train!' my big brother shouted, his voice sharp with urgency.

I grabbed the last of my things, heart thudding in my chest. The morning had arrived – but was I really ready? This felt massive. Like a point of no return.

C'mon, Ricky, you can do this. I swallowed hard, tossing back one last handful of prescription pills I'd coaxed from my GP. Heroin? Check. Valium? Check. More than enough to get me through the journey.

'Ricky, come on, bro!' his voice cut through my thoughts again, this time with more frustration.

'That's me! Let's do this, bro!' I called back, casting one final look at my flat. Closing the door felt like sealing off a chapter I'd barely survived.

At the train station, he pulled me into a hug, eyes glassy. 'I know you can do this, bro. We're all so proud of you.'

'Thanks, bro. I'm sorry for everything – for the mess I got into. But I'm so grateful you and the rest of the family never gave up on me, even at my worst.'

'Always, bro.' He held me for a second longer, then let go. 'Now hurry up – you'd better catch that train.'

As the train pulled away, I slumped into a seat and felt the weight of it all. Doubt began creeping in. My mind spiralled. Just one last blowout before it all ends. Numbing the fear, I made my way to the toilet, took more drugs, and let the high settle in.

By the time I reached Swansea, I was completely off my face. Someone from Teen Challenge was there to meet me – a staff member with a kind face – but the whole thing passed in a blur. I barely remembered the car ride. I barely remembered arriving.

That first night? Gone.

But the next morning . . . that's when the reality of what I'd signed up for came crashing in.

***

'Ricky . . . Ricky . . . RICKY . . . it's time to get up!'

A man's voice pierced through the fog in my mind.

'What . . . what is it?' I croaked, my head pounding, the last traces of the previous day's drugs still clinging to me like a heavy blanket.

'It's time to get up, Ricky. Chapel starts in five minutes.'

'Chapel?' I mumbled, blinking against the blur of morning light.

'All residents attend chapel every morning,' he replied, far too upbeat for the hour.

I rubbed my face. 'Can I get my meds first?'

'Yes, I'll sort them if you get up now.'

That was all the motivation I needed. The thought of relief jolted me upright. My body craved the comfort of detox medication like a drowning man reaching for a life ring.

I stumbled downstairs, nerves creeping in as I realised I was about to face the rest of the centre for the first time – at least in a state where I might actually remember it.

I entered the chapel and froze. The place was alive. Chatter filled the air, the buzz of people who somehow seemed . . . hopeful. A live band kicked off – guitars, keyboard, even drums. In a church? My only reference point was funerals or old women singing hymns off-key. This felt more like a gig than a chapel service.

Then it happened.

The room erupted. Thirty or forty people, most of them residents, were suddenly on their feet, hands raised, voices lifted. Some prayed out loud. Others cried. Their passion was overwhelming.

What are they reaching for? I thought, bewildered. I looked up at the ceiling instinctively, as if the answer might be hovering there.

A strange tightness wrapped around my chest. My breathing quickened. My skin prickled. I didn't know what I was feeling, but I didn't like it.

The intensity felt suffocating. My mind reeled. *What have I got myself into this time?* Overwhelmed, I dropped my head into my hands, my breath shallow. A tear slipped down my cheek before I even realised it. I felt trapped, drowning in emotions I couldn't name.

I couldn't stay.

Heart thudding, I jumped up and rushed out of the room.

A staff member caught up with me. 'Are you OK, Ricky?' he asked gently.

'No, I'm not,' I snapped. 'I'm going to my room.'

I didn't wait for a response. I just needed to escape.

Back in my room, I slammed the door and leaned against it, trying to calm my breathing. My mind was spinning.

Welcome to Teen Challenge, I thought anxiously.

This place wasn't just a rehab centre. It was something else. Something intense. Bootcamp meets church. And I wasn't sure I was ready for either.

***

I had definitely started the programme with a bang. After my dramatic chapel exit, I expected to be left alone to recover – but no such luxury. This place didn't mess about. While the induction phase gave you a bit of leeway to adjust – like more rest and lighter duties – you were still expected to engage with the structure of the day. And trust me, the structure was relentless.

They had a daily timetable pinned to the noticeboard that read like something out of the military:

7:15am	Wake up, showers, clean rooms
7:45am	Morning devotions
8:00am	Breakfast
8:30am	Washing-up and house duties
9:30am	Church service
10:00am	Class time
10:45am	Coffee break
11:15am	Class continues
12:30pm	Lunch and clean-up
1:30pm	Afternoon work programme
5:00pm	Free time
5:30pm	Evening meal and clean-up

7:00pm	Evening studies (*in silence!*)
8:30pm	Free time
10:00pm	Evening prayers
10:30pm	In rooms
10:45pm	Lights out

During those first few weeks, I wasn't thrown into the full workload, but I still had to show up to chapel, devotions, and a few duties – enough to realise what I'd signed up for. No lying-in till noon. No drifting through the day on my own terms. This was a full-on environment designed to shake you out of your old life and snap you into a new rhythm.

It was jarring. I'd gone from living chaotically and doing whatever I wanted, whenever I wanted, to being told when to eat, pray, study, clean, and even when to go to bed. It felt like rehab by stopwatch.

At first, I hated it. The order, the rules, the routine. I was used to numbing out and floating through life. Now, I had to show up – even if just halfway – for things I didn't understand, alongside people I didn't yet trust.

But even in that limited engagement, something about the routine started to ground me. My body was still in withdrawal, my emotions all over the place. And as much as I wanted to rebel against the structure, a small part of me knew – I needed it.

***

'Teen Challenge?' one of the lads scoffed, his voice dripping with sarcasm. 'Sounds more like an adventure playground for wayward teenagers.'

It was only his second day in the programme, and already he'd become the loudest voice in the induction group. He sat in the common room, feet up on the table, holding court with a handful of other new residents. I hovered at the edge, still finding my bearings.

'You'd think there'd at least be a jacuzzi for the withdrawals,' he went on, rolling his eyes. 'Maybe a steam room. Maybe even a five-a-side league for our "emotional needs".' The room erupted in laughter.

I cracked a half-smile, but inside, I was still reeling. Nothing could've prepared me for the intensity of this place. No one here was tiptoeing around addiction recovery. There were no softly-softly therapy sessions. No comfy sofas and soothing mantras. This place was raw. Honest. Relentless.

I'd been warned the programme wasn't easy. But it wasn't until I got inside that I realised what 'challenge' really meant. The success rate here – 70 to 80 per cent for those who finished – spoke volumes. But finishing? That was the real test.

I had a strong will, sure. I wasn't a quitter. But the environment had a way of pressing every button, exposing every weakness. The people who really bought into the programme – especially those who were serious about their faith – they baffled me.

They weren't just clean. They were different. Gentle but strong. Kind, but not soft. Confident, but not arrogant. There was a peace about them that made me uncomfortable. It didn't make sense.

I naturally gravitated towards the sceptics – the comedians, the streetwise lads who still carried the same hardness I did. Within two weeks, I'd already landed myself in trouble. My first 'put-back' – basically a penalty where you lost progress in the programme. It was like having a last-minute winning goal disallowed. Brutal.

They called it 'chosen but frozen' – when your journey stalls because your heart's not in it. And mine? It was definitely still divided.

But even as I played the part of the lad, running with the wrong crew, I couldn't help noticing the difference in the guys who'd gone all in with God. They weren't faking it. You couldn't fake that kind of peace.

And somewhere deep inside, I knew – I wanted what they had.

***

The detox lead didn't look like someone who'd been on drugs. That's what threw a lot of the lads. He was calm, well put together, and had a good sense of humour – but he didn't let anyone get away with nonsense. You wouldn't pick him out as someone with a past like ours, but he didn't hide it either. He carried himself with quiet confidence, and most of the lads – whether they admitted it or not – respected him for it. He'd been through this very programme years earlier and now ran the detox unit. There was no front with him. Just honesty, consistency, and a no-nonsense approach.

Still, not everyone appreciated that.

'Did you hear?' someone muttered over a mug of lukewarm tea, frustration simmering just beneath his voice.

'Hear what?' I asked.

'About him,' another jumped in before the first could answer, his tone thick with sarcasm. 'He used to be on gear, same as us.'

I raised an eyebrow. 'Seriously?'

'Oh aye,' he continued, winding up. 'Now he walks about like he owns the place – telling folk what to do, acting like he's never touched the stuff.'

'He doesn't act like that,' another lad chipped in from across the room. 'He's just got standards. The guy's been clean for years – he's trying to help us.'

The cynic scoffed. 'Help us? Please. He's only just out the other side himself. Now he's strutting around like he's the poster boy for recovery. It's all a bit much, mate.'

'Maybe he just doesn't want to end up back where he came from,' the other lad offered. 'He's not pretending to be perfect – he's just not playing games.'

A glare was shot across the room. 'Easy for him now though, eh? He's done his time. But don't forget – he was where we are. He should know how hard this is, instead of barking orders and acting all holier-than-thou.'

The one defending him stood his ground. 'You don't have to like him, but you can't deny he's walking it out. His faith's genuine. That's more than most.'

A snort came from another corner. 'Careful – bit rich coming from someone who's been on more recovery programmes than hot dinners.'

He didn't rise to it. 'Maybe that's why you should listen. I've learned the hard way.'

'Spare us the wisdom, mate. Nobody's listening.'

But I was.

I watched how the detox lead carried himself. Steady. Kind, but clear. He didn't just talk about freedom – he lived it. And something about that unsettled me . . . in a good way.

***

'Is there anyone here who doesn't know Jesus?' the detox leader asked, his voice steady but full of urgency. We'd just finished a deep discussion, but now he was cutting to the heart.

'What do you mean?' one of the lads asked, frowning.

He leaned forward. 'Have you ever said a prayer of salvation? Have you ever invited Jesus into your life?'

The room fell still. Eyes flicked sideways. No one wanted to be the first to speak. After a pause, he stood up.

'I'm heading to the chapel. If anyone wants to join me, I'd be honoured to pray with you.'

Then he walked out – simple as that.

A few guys glanced at each other. One stood. Then another. The rest of us sat rooted in place. I didn't move. But I couldn't stop thinking about it.

That night, sleep wouldn't come. With my detox meds being cut down, I was already restless. But now my thoughts were spinning.

Could I really become a Christian? Was that even possible for someone like me?

I remembered the peace in the guys who'd gone all in – their quiet confidence, their freedom. And something in me cracked open.

Maybe I needed what they had?

I started reading the Bible every chance I got. The words stirred something I couldn't explain. Until finally, I knew – I had to speak to him.

'All right, Ricky?' he said as I approached.

I swallowed hard. 'Would you . . . would you pray with me? To become a Christian?'

A wide smile spread across his face. 'I'd be honoured, mate.'

He led me to the chapel. It was quiet. Still. As if heaven itself was holding its breath.

We sat near the front, and he placed a hand on my shoulder.

'Just repeat after me. Pray it like you mean it.'

I nodded, heart thudding.

He began slowly:

'Lord Jesus, I know that I've messed up. I've sinned. And I can't fix it on my own.

'I believe you are the Son of God, that you died for me, and rose again.

'I'm asking you now – please forgive me.

'Come into my life.

'Fill me with your Spirit.

'Give me the strength to live for you from this day forward.

'I give you everything.

'Thank you for saving me. Amen.'

As I repeated each line, my voice shook. I didn't understand everything. But I meant it. And in that moment, something changed.

It wasn't loud. It wasn't dramatic.

But it was real.

I'd said yes to Jesus.

And I would never be the same.

***

Despite the spiritual shift I had just experienced, life without drugs was still a daily battle. Eight weeks in, and I had completed my detox – my body was finally clear of substances for the first time in years.

But instead of feeling free, I felt . . . lost.

Who even am I? I stared at my reflection in the oversized mirror, my twenty-eight-year-old self looking back at me, unfamiliar and hollow.

Without heroin to numb the pain, without Valium to quiet my thoughts, without alcohol to mask the anxiety – what was left? I had no idea how to sit with myself. No idea how to feel normal.

For years, those substances had been my escape, my armour, my identity. And now, stripped of them, I felt completely exposed.

The struggle wasn't just physical anymore. It was emotional. Mental. Spiritual. My lack of self-awareness, self-confidence, and, above all, self-acceptance began to feel like the biggest giants I'd ever faced.

And then came the blow.

'Ricky, we can't go on like this anymore,' the centre manager said one afternoon, his voice steady but firm. 'Whenever there's trouble, you and your group aren't far from it.'

I froze. 'What do you mean?' I asked, already knowing.

He gave me a long look. 'I'm going to have to ask you to leave.'

It hit me like a punch to the gut.

'What? What do you mean leave? I can't go home – I'm not ready,' I pleaded.

'You've been here six months and have only just reached Phase Two. You've had multiple put-backs and lost nearly half your progress.'

My heart sank. 'Please . . . I know I've messed up, but if I go home now, I'll go straight back to Valium. I'll drink. It'll all spiral again – I know it will.'

He didn't say anything at first, just studied me.

Then I offered the only sliver of hope I had: 'Is there any chance – any chance at all – you could phone one of the other centres? Maybe see if they'd take me?'

He sighed, rubbed his chin, then finally nodded. 'Wait outside while I make the call. But if I do this, I need your word that you'll commit. Are you ready for that?'

'I am. I will. I promise.'

I waited, nerves coiled tight in my stomach.

Eventually, the door opened.

'Alright, Ricky. Go pack your things. You're going to London.'

'London?' I repeated, stunned.

'Yes. But you'll be back to the beginning of Phase One.'

'The beginning of Phase One? That's like being four weeks into the programme!' I protested.

'Yes,' he confirmed. 'But that's their condition. Take it or leave it.'

I exhaled sharply, then nodded. 'Okay, I'll do it. Thanks again for sorting this.'

'Don't let me down, Ricky. Now go pack. We're taking you straight to the train station.'

I left the room and quietly began packing.

A new chapter was about to begin.

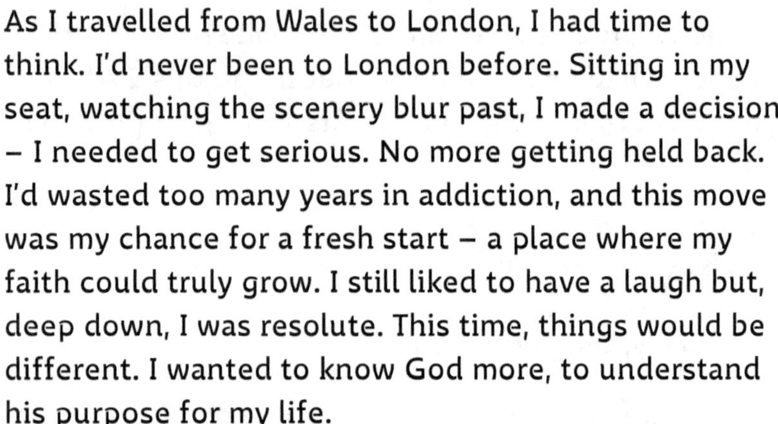

As I travelled from Wales to London, I had time to think. I'd never been to London before. Sitting in my seat, watching the scenery blur past, I made a decision – I needed to get serious. No more getting held back. I'd wasted too many years in addiction, and this move was my chance for a fresh start – a place where my faith could truly grow. I still liked to have a laugh but, deep down, I was resolute. This time, things would be different. I wanted to know God more, to understand his purpose for my life.

One of my first real encounters with God came towards the end of 2007, not long after I arrived in London. Each Sunday, Teen Challenge took us to a local church, and it was there, during one of those services, that the pastor prayed for me and said, 'I see a treasure chest that the devil has kept locked for years. Inside are many treasures – gifts and abilities God has given you. God is opening that chest now, and the devil will no longer keep it closed.'

Something in me shifted. Those words resonated deeply. Addiction had stolen my confidence, leaving me hopeless about the future, but now . . . now I felt something stirring. Maybe, just maybe, God had a plan for me after all.

After six months in London, I was seriously considering my future post-rehab. Phase Four of the programme – the re-entry phase – was approaching, and I had to decide what came next. University seemed like a logical step. It had been five years since I'd completed my degree, and with technology evolving fast, a refresher course in multimedia made sense.

But something inside me said I needed to pray first.

That night, before bed, I got on my knees. *God, should I go back to university or not?* I asked sincerely.

To my surprise, I received an answer in a dream.

In the dream, a pitch-black background appeared, and bold white writing scrolled across the screen:

> '"But seek first his kingdom and his righteousness, and all these things will be given to you as well"
>
> *(Matthew 6:33)*.'

I jolted awake, the words ringing in my mind. I wasn't even that familiar with Bible verses, let alone their locations, but I grabbed the Bible next to my bed. When I found the scripture, my heart pounded. The exact words from my dream were there on the page.

This was an answer from God.

But did I listen?

I had been praying about university, but also about a wife, a good job, a house, a car – things I believed

God wanted for me. But that verse made it clear: I was getting it the wrong way round. God wasn't saying those things were wrong – he was saying they shouldn't come first.

I needed to seek him first. His kingdom. His righteousness.

But despite receiving such a clear answer, I chose to pursue university. I applied and was accepted. On paper, it made sense. But deep down, I knew I was putting my agenda ahead of God's. I wasn't seeking *him* first – I was chasing the life I wanted, hoping he'd bless it as I went.

***

'Ricky, unless you sort out your attitude and behaviours, you're going to relapse.'

I felt the heat rise in my face. 'How dare you say that!' I snapped.

The director of Teen Challenge London remained calm, unfazed. 'Ricky, we've seen it all before. The warning signs are clear.'

His gaze was steady – almost too steady.

'You've been on Phase Four for three months now, and it's clear you've been putting most of your energy into your university course. We feel it's time for you to move on.'

The words hit me like a ton of bricks. I wanted to argue, to tell them they were wrong. But deep down, a part of me knew they weren't.

I clenched my fists, forcing myself to stay composed.

The centre manager stepped in, handing me an envelope. 'We've written a letter confirming you've completed a year in the Teen Challenge programme. Take this to the local council – they'll prioritise you for housing.'

I took the letter, nodding stiffly. 'Thanks,' I muttered, though my chest burned with frustration.

I'd started university during Phase Four, thinking I could juggle both worlds – faith and future, calling and control. But if I was honest, I'd poured far more of myself into education than transformation.

How could they say I was going to relapse? I was fine. I had my plans. I had my future mapped out.

But as I walked away, their words echoed louder than I cared to admit – soon, they'd become a reality I couldn't outrun.

Chapter 6

Hurry Up and Die . . .

'Ricky! Great to hear from you, bro! What you up to? Where are you now?' Colin's voice burst through the phone, full of excitement. We hadn't spoken in ages.

Sheepishly, I replied, 'That's me out, man. Finished rehab. Can't believe I was in there for eighteen months!'

'What?!' Colin practically shouted. 'You were in there that long? That's more like a jail sentence!' He laughed. 'What was it like? Worse than the jail?'

I chuckled. 'Well . . . in some ways, aye. No smoking, no TV – it wasn't what I expected. But, man, it changed my life.'

'Well done, bro. Proud of you. No many people from Hawick sort themselves oot like you have,' he said, his voice turning serious for a moment.

A brief silence followed as we both let the thought sink in.

'Anyway . . . what you up to now? Where are you?'

'London, bro.'

'London?! What you doin' in the big smoke, man? Thought you went to Wales?'

'Long story, bro. Got transferred to their London rehab, finished a couple months ago. I'm in a homeless hotel, waiting for my own flat. But it's not as bad as it sounds. I've been doing okay. Still off the gear.'

'Well done, mate. Proud o' ya. No easy to get off and stay off the gear.'

'Aye, I know.' I hesitated. 'I've been having a wee drink now and again. With Christmas coming up, I wanted to ask you a favour.'

'Of course, bro. What is it?'

'Well . . . you got any Valium?'

Colin laughed. 'Of course I do. You know me. You sure, though? After rehab and all that?'

'Aye, bro.' I quickly brushed off his concern. 'You still do the deal for a hundred?'

'For you? Aye, of course! Text me your address, and I'll get them to you today.'

'Thanks, bro. Hopefully we can catch up when I'm next up seeing my maw.'

'That'd be good, bro. Take it easy.'

'You too,' I said, hanging up.

The council had placed me in the Ashfield Road 'Hotel' in Ilford, a homeless hostel. At first, I kept to myself, focusing on my studies. But as Christmas neared, I felt the pull of my old ways.

The craving hit me hard. I had already started drinking occasionally and smoking again. My old mindset crept back in. I knew where Valium could take me, but the longing for that familiar numbness was overwhelming. *Why pay over the odds for a few when I could get a good deal on a hundred?* It was a crazy idea, but I called Colin anyway.

A few days later, they arrived. As I swallowed the first few, the warmth I had been craving surged through me. But the comfort was fleeting. Within a week, I had taken them all, mixing them with alcohol – my old favourite concoction. Blackouts followed, entire days lost. People I had been avoiding suddenly approached me, recounting things I had done, things I couldn't remember.

A whole new world had reopened, and soon, I found myself smoking crack in the hotel. That was when I met Matt, who lived a few doors down.

It wasn't long before I crossed the final line, where my addiction reached depths I had never known.

***

'Take off your belt,' Matt instructed, his voice flat, almost detached. 'Wrap it round your upper arm and pull it tight. Make sure the veins pop.'

My heart pounded. A twisted cocktail of dread and anticipation surged through me. For years, I'd told myself I'd never cross this line. I'd watched others do it. Judged them even. But now . . . here I was.

About to inject for the first time.

And not just heroin. A snowball – heroin and crack cocaine. A cocktail for chaos.

Perched on the edge of the bed, I watched Matt move like he'd done this a hundred times. He melted the substances together in a battered spoon, flame dancing beneath it, the dark liquid swirling into readiness. He drew the mixture up into a syringe with practised ease.

'Relax,' he said. 'I've done this loads o' times.'

I said nothing. Just clenched my fist.

He found the vein, drew a little blood, then slowly pushed the syringe in.

And then – wave after wave of warm euphoria crashed through me. It was heavier, deeper, darker than anything I'd ever felt.

The next thing I remember, I was blinking.

Dazed.

Matt was leaning over me, voice tight with urgency. 'Ricky, wake up! You alright, bruv?'

'Yeah . . . I think so. What just happened?' My voice was slurred.

'You overdosed,' he said, wide-eyed. 'You went under. I thought you were done for.'

He reached for something on the floor. 'Look – I recorded it.'

He shoved my phone into my hands.

I squinted at the screen, the image bouncing and shaky.

It was him – in panic. Screaming.

'WAKE UP!'

I froze. My blood turned cold.

This was it. The bed in the video. The marks on the walls. The threadbare carpet underfoot. It had all happened right here.

Same room. Same moment. Same bed.

And the lifeless body on the bed – the pale skin, blue-tinged lips – it was me.

He'd filmed it.

'I had to,' Matt said quickly. 'I thought you were gone. I didn't know what to do.'

I couldn't speak. Watching yourself look dead is not something you ever prepare for.

'I gave you CPR,' he added, almost as an afterthought.

I nodded slowly. But I was still trying to make sense of what I'd seen.

And then he dropped the line that chilled me even more than the footage.

'This ain't the first time I've had to bring someone back.'

I looked at him sharply.

His gaze had drifted to the far wall.

'Get a grip,' he suddenly muttered. 'Get a grip, lad.'

He paced the room like something inside him had been unchained.

'It's sick . . . sick, that's what it is. I'm not takin' the blame, not again!'

His voice got quicker, jumpy. He looked at me, eyes darting. 'Nope, weren't my fault – not this time. Couldn't do nothin'. Nothin' I could've done.'

He was trying to convince me – but mostly, it seemed, trying to convince himself.

'It's like some twisted nightmare,' he rambled. 'Had me whole life ahead o' me, and this fella goes and ruins it by dying . . .'

He let out a shaky laugh.

'Fools. They all blamed me.'

I stayed silent. Let him talk. My head was still spinning from what I'd seen.

Matt's hand gestured wildly as he continued, 'A right travesty-of-justic-carrige, that's what it was!'

'A what?'

'A travesty-of-justic-carrige,' he repeated, sulking.

'You mean a miscarriage of justice?'

'That's what I said!'

'Right . . .'

'Scandalous, it was. A tragedy of justice, carriage-style,' he mumbled, lost in his own theatre of self-defence. 'Not my fault, never was . . .'

He kept pacing, twitching, blinking, whispering things I couldn't quite catch. But every now and then, fragments drifted clear.

'I only gave him the booster. The gear was solid, the hit was clean. And I helped, yeah? Just tried to help.'

He paused, then added, 'Then the police kicked the door in. That's when I got nicked.'

'So . . . you went down for giving someone a bad hit?' I asked, cautiously.

He glanced at the floor. His tone dropped.

'Well . . . and for leaving the body in a cupboard.'

My breath caught. 'What?'

'Yeah. Got it in one,' he said with an odd shrug. 'Got banged up, didn't I? Back inside. Just for helpin' a mate.'

I stared at him, stunned.

'I mean . . . what kind of person . . .' I started.

But he was off again.

'So, this guy – he goes over after a dig, right? So we puts him in the cupboard. Thought he was just out cold, like usual. He hated bein' woken up after a hit – used to go off on one if he got disturbed.'

He paused, almost like he was remembering an old mate with fondness.

'Once I woke him too early – nearly took my head off,' he chuckled. 'Pardon the pun.'

Then his tone shifted, more matter-of-fact than remorseful.

'But yeah . . . truth is, we were on it for days after. Didn't even think. Out our heads, totally. Higher than a pilot's packed lunch, we were. Forgot he was even in there.'

He looked away, scratching at his wrist.

'It was a neighbour, see. Clocked the smell. Said it was off – proper bad. Called the old bill. They kicked the door in, found him still in the cupboard . . .'

He shrugged, as if that explained everything.

'Next thing I know, I'm in cuffs. Said I left him there like some kind of monster. But I never meant for none of it. I was just off me nut, mate. That's all.'

He said it all like he was recounting a heavy weekend – not someone's death.

'Nobody was more gutted than me to lose him,' he added, shaking his head. 'But I know he's up there lookin' down sayin', "Not your fault. Not your fault at all . . ."'

I nodded solemnly, though everything in me was recoiling.

Inside, I was cringing – at him, at myself, at how far I'd fallen.

***

Would this be the scare that finally woke me up? That brought me back to the flicker of hope I'd glimpsed less than two years earlier?

Sadly, no.

My descent wasn't over. Not yet. For now it continued . . .

I sat there for a long time after he finally went quiet. The room around me felt smaller somehow, heavier. The smell of stale smoke clung to the curtains, and that tea-stained wall across from me seemed to stare back. It was the same wall I'd seen in the video – just a few feet behind that pale, lifeless body. I didn't need anyone to tell me. I already knew. I'd been that close to leaving this world. Closer than ever. And somehow . . . I was still here.

But why?

***

'What on earth is he banging on about? This is absolutely mad,' I muttered under my breath as my drugs worker once again went on about this strange 'pink elephant' recovery movement. His enthusiasm was relentless, but I just wasn't buying it.

'Look, I know this has helped you in your own recovery, but this is not me,' I sighed, lowering my head, staring at the floor between my legs.

Lifting my gaze, eyes narrowed, I continued, 'You know faith-based recovery is my thing. But like I've told you before, I'm not going back to Teen Challenge. What about the detox unit in Central London you were trying to get me into? Any luck?'

'Well, sorry, mate,' he stuttered in his thick East London accent, 'the demand is high . . . but what about the pink–'

'Don't go there!' I snapped, frustration bubbling over. 'I've been waiting months! Someone told me you got him a place, and he came to you after I did! What's that about?'

'Well, I–' He looked away, breaking eye contact.

I exhaled sharply. 'I need to go. Just write my prescription,' I said, standing abruptly. 'I need the loo.'

'Okay, no problem.'

As I collected my methadone and diazepam script, shame settled in my gut like a stone. How had I ended up here? I would never have injected or gone on methadone back home. Now, I was worse than ever.

Trying to push the thought aside, I turned my attention back to him. Stupid pink elephant movement. What is that guy on? Shaking my head, I fumed over someone else getting a place before me. Did he like him better or something?

Then, like a lightning bolt, the thought struck: *There is one door open for you, and one door only.*

Instantly, I knew what it meant. Teen Challenge.

No chance, I thought bitterly. *There's no way I'm going back there.*

But the thought wouldn't leave me, and I was reminded of a recent encounter . . .

'Ricky – how you doing?' a voice called out as I walked through Ilford town centre.

Turning, my stomach sank. It was someone I knew from rehab.

'What you up to? Haven't seen you since you left Teen Challenge.'

'I've got my own flat now, and I'm in my third year at East London University,' I replied quickly, trying to mask the mess my life had become.

'Aw, that's great. Well done.' His words were kind, but his eyes told me he knew the truth.

'You still in church?' he asked.

'Aye, I go to King's Church.'

Here it comes. The question I knew was coming.

'You don't look too good. I heard you're back using.'

'Aye, but it's not too bad. I'll sort it,' I said, feigning control.

'What about coming back to Teen Challenge?'

'No,' I shot back. 'No, I don't need another programme. Anyway, nice to see you,' I added hastily, turning on my heel.

I needed to get away. Fast.

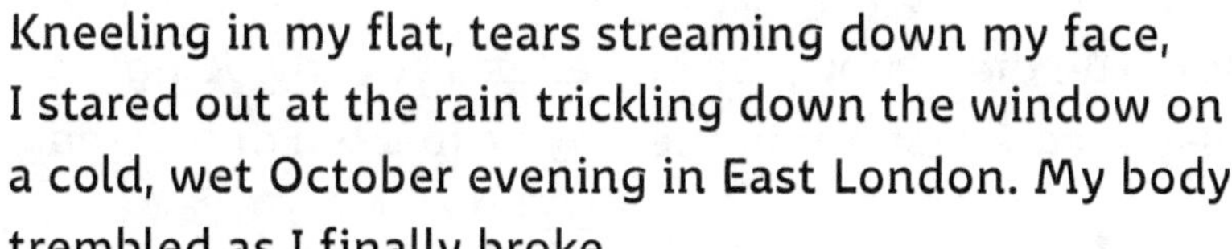

Kneeling in my flat, tears streaming down my face, I stared out at the rain trickling down the window on a cold, wet October evening in East London. My body trembled as I finally broke.

'God, I can't do this any more!' I cried out, my voice raw with desperation.

My gaze dropped to my left arm, watching the angry lump swell even further. Shaking my head, I buried it in my hands, sobs wracking my body. Outside, the wind howled through the streets, an eerie darkness closing in, mirroring the storm inside my soul.

'Take everything . . .' I whispered, my voice barely audible through my tears. 'I'll do whatever you want me to do – even if it means quitting university and going back to Teen Challenge. I just can't take this any more.'

My reddened eyes caught sight of the needle lying on the floor beside me. Disgust twisted in my gut. I tilted my head towards the ceiling, my voice breaking, 'Lord, please help me.'

My drug use had spiralled completely out of control. Injecting 'snowballs' had become my norm, but this time I had missed the vein, leaving an abscess bulging on my left arm. I felt utterly lost, drowning in the silence that followed my plea. The absence of an immediate answer only deepened my despair.

But little did I know, my prayer was already being answered – just not in the way I expected or wanted.

Something had shifted. Though nothing outwardly changed, I had reached a place of true surrender.
I was now in my final year at the University of East London, and quitting had never been my style.
My determination had always pushed me through adversity. But this time, I knew I couldn't keep going on my own.

At my lowest, I was reminded of the dream I'd had in Teen Challenge. I had spent years chasing fulfilment in the wrong places. Since 1998, I hadn't stayed in one place longer than three years. I kept convincing myself that if I moved here, got this qualification, landed that job, things would change.

But they never did.

Because the problem wasn't external. It was within me. It was a heart issue.

Realising this, I finally gave in to what I had been resisting. I contacted Teen Challenge London, completed an application, and was placed on the waiting list for their programme in Wales.

Six months passed between that moment of surrender and re-entering Teen Challenge Wales in May 2010. Looking back, I see now that God had been leading me all along, stripping away my false hopes. The life I had been searching for could only be found in surrendering to him.

This was the lesson that would change everything – the key to the transformation I had been longing for.

Chapter 7

First Fruits of Surrender

So here I was, back where my rehab journey had begun three years earlier. In one sense, I was 'back to square one', but in reality, I was a completely different person from the man who first walked through these doors. The past three years had been a rollercoaster of highs and lows, and through it all, God had been working in my life, bringing me to that place of surrender.

During detox, I found myself standing in front of the same oversized mirror I had stared into the first time I was here. Back then, I hadn't recognised the man staring back at me – stripped of substances, I had felt lost, hollow. But this time, I smiled at my reflection. No more masks. No more pretence. I could finally just be me.

A wave of relief washed over me. Self-acceptance – something I had never truly grasped – now felt within reach. It was this realisation, this surrender to

God's will, that had changed me. After eight weeks, my detox was complete, and I sensed in my heart that something significant had shifted. It was a sweet, victorious moment, hard-earned through pain and adversity.

How often do we have to go through suffering to learn the lessons God wants to teach us?

Looking in that mirror, I could now meet my own gaze without shame. The weight of past failures – the 'hurts, hang-ups and habits' that had haunted me – no longer held power over my emotions, my mind or my will. I was free.

I can just be me.

But as I stood there, another realisation dawned – not about the drugs, but about what had been buried beneath them all along.

The drugs had only ever been the surface issue.

Yes, I hoped I might finally break free from heroin and diazepam. But deep down, I believed I would always carry the shame, guilt and pain of my past. That I'd never truly escape the depression, anxiety and inner torment that had defined so much of my life.

But something was different now.

Through classes like *Loving and Accepting Myself*, and through coming to a place of full surrender to the will of God, those old chains had finally begun to break. I didn't need to carry that weight anymore. Christ had already carried it for me.

I didn't need to earn my worth. I didn't need to fix myself.

I was already loved. Already forgiven. Already free.

Free to be me – the man God had created me to be.

And that was totally liberating. Totally transformational.

Like a shattered mirror pieced back together, I knew the cracks in my past no longer defined me – they had become marks of grace.

The more I remembered my salvation, the more I realised my life wasn't about me – it was about him. 'He must become greater; I must become less' (John 3:30).

For the first time, I could simply be who God made me to be. No masks. No striving. Just a life built on Christ.

God's grace hadn't just carried me – it had conquered.

What I once saw as defeat, he had been using all along to prepare me. Every failure, every fall, now part of the story he was redeeming for his purpose.

'You know who you are,' the teacher said.

It was during one of the evening classes the programme offered that my calling to leadership was both ignited and confirmed.

Our eyes met across the room in that awkward, unspoken way we've all experienced – as if something had just been agreed without words. But it wasn't until his next words that everything sharpened into focus.

'Some of you are called to leadership.'

In that moment, something shifted deep within me. A certainty – a quiet but unshakeable knowing – settled in my soul. Theology might call it an *ontological shift* – a change in being. Or as we say in Scotland, *'It's mair felt than telt.'*

I knew it was the Holy Spirit. Not just guiding me as he had done so many times before, but now empowering me. I could feel him affirming something I hadn't dared to believe – that God was not only calling me, but equipping me. That inner power, which I now understood was the Spirit at work, began to rise within.

Could this be one of the treasures the devil had tried to keep locked away all those years? One that God was now releasing?

For the first time, I didn't just dream – I believed. Not in myself, but in what God could do through me.

I – even I – had a leadership calling.

You are not just here for yourself.

The timing of those words was like a tonic to my soul. They surfaced in my mind as I wandered through the back garden of the rehab centre one warm summer evening. A heavy despondency had begun to settle in as the reality of completing yet another full programme dawned on me.

Do I really have another programme in me? Do I need to go through the whole thing again? The questions circled relentlessly, doubt creeping in.

Then, like a ton of bricks, those words hit me.

It was exactly what I needed to hear. In that instant, something shifted. My perspective began to change, pulling me out of self-pity and turning my focus outward. God was showing me that this journey wasn't just about me – it was about others too.

I started noticing those who struggled to adapt, those who felt lost in the routine of rehab. And instead of just focusing on myself, I began looking for ways to help. This wasn't just about my recovery; it was about serving, supporting, and encouraging those walking the same difficult road.

Up to this point, it had all been about me. My recovery. My journey. I had been so selfish.

This shift marked the beginning of my ministry – my first real training ground in helping others.

And because of the deeper transformation I had undergone since my first time at the centre, I'm glad to say that I completed the programme this time without any put-backs. Now, it was time to move on to the next stage of my journey.

***

The leader's strong Northern Irish accent cut through the noise of Swansea city centre. She pointed to a dejected man sitting on the pavement, begging.

She was bold, passionate, and unwavering – the head of Teen Challenge's School of Ministry training, where graduates learned how to work with people in addiction. I had just started the course, and it was already pushing me out of my comfort zone.

'Right, go over and speak to that man,' she said, eyes fixed on me.

'What, me?' I blurted out, caught off guard.

'Yes, you,' she replied firmly, then waved over one of the more experienced members of the team. 'He'll go with you – he's done plenty of street outreach.'

My stomach twisted as the two of us began walking towards the man, my mind racing with doubts.

What if he gets upset? Swears at us? Or worse . . . what if he tries to hit one of us? My heart pounded. I had never done anything like this before.

Reaching the man, I hesitated, then looked to my partner. 'On you go, bro – you're the expert here!' I said, half-joking, hoping he'd take the lead.

But as conversation after conversation unfolded, my fears slowly dissolved. Most people were open, receptive, even grateful for the chat. Yes, some weren't interested, but the hostility I had dreaded was rare. Each interaction built my confidence, and, with every step, I felt something awaken in me.

Little did I know, this would be the beginning of my love affair with street outreach ministry.

Ask him to pray for a double portion of his leadership anointing.

Lying in the back of the pickup truck, I gazed out at the endless rows of cold, grey concrete flats lining the highway – a stark reminder of Romania's communist past. The night's outreach in Bucharest played over in my mind, and I couldn't shake how deeply impressed I had been by the leader. His passion, his leadership, the way he engaged people of all ages with such warmth and authority – it stirred something inside me.

Our mission trip had taken us into one of the darkest places imaginable – an underground world where kids lived in sewers. It sounded horrific, and in many ways it was. We had ventured into tunnels thick with darkness, littered with used needles. But in the main sewer systems, we found an entire hidden society – well-lit tunnels warmed by huge hot-water pipes, where makeshift communities had formed. Young teens, barely old enough to fend for themselves, were leading these networks. It was heart-breaking.

And yet, amidst the tragedy, there were moments of joy. One of our team members, always the joker, decided the best approach was to simply have fun. A dance-off broke out – laughter echoing through the tunnels. For that brief moment, the heaviness lifted and I knew the kids would remember it.

The leader guided the outreach with such power and love, and as we travelled back to our accommodation, the thought gripped me: *Ask him to pray for a double portion of his leadership anointing.*

I had been reading in the Bible, where Elisha asks Elijah for a double portion of his spirit before he is taken away.[7] That passage came alive in my spirit as I reflected on the calling I felt stirring within me.

As we pulled up, the team climbed out, thanking him for the evening. I hung back. My heart pounded as I approached him.

'I was really inspired by what I saw tonight – especially your leadership and the way you connected with

7. 2 Kings 2:9–10.

people. While lying in the back of your pickup, I felt led to ask – would you pray for me? That God would give me a double portion of your leadership anointing?'

A slow smile spread across his face. 'I'd be delighted to. Let's pray.'

Placing his hands firmly on my shoulders, he lifted his voice to God, asking him to pour out his anointing over my life and grant my request.

Not long after, I was reminded of another moment – back in Wales, during a leadership training session. After one of the teachings, the speaker approached me and another student, saying he felt led to pray for us – to pass on a leadership anointing.

I knew this was no coincidence. This was confirmation.

God was calling me. And I truly believe something powerful was imparted to me in those moments of prayer.

***

Before I was ready for any leadership position, God had some key lessons to teach me first.

On my laptop, I had loads of copied music and software. I hadn't thought much of it – until now. Many of the junior staff and men on the latter stages of the programme would swap copied Christian music, something I was beginning to feel convicted about.

One day, someone approached me.

'I hear you have some good Christian music. Can you make me a copy?'

'Um . . . no . . . sorry, I can't,' I hesitated.

'What? Why not?' he snapped, clearly annoyed.

'I can't. I've been feeling convicted about it all.'

'Don't get all super-spiritual on me. It's fine – it's Christian!'

'Exactly!' I exclaimed. 'Isn't that even more of a reason why we shouldn't be doing it? And anyway, I'm going to delete all my music off my computer.'

'Whatever, man,' he scoffed, shaking his head as he walked away.

That evening, I sat at my laptop, feeling a mix of determination and trepidation. As I dragged the music folder to the recycle bin, I was surprised at how difficult it was to follow through.

Phew, that was tougher than I thought, I admitted to myself. But almost instantly, I felt a deep sense of relief and joy.

Then came another challenge.

Just as I started rebuilding my music collection the right way, another thought hit me: *What about the copied software?*

My heart sank.

No, not the software! What if I need this?

I had pirated copies of all the Adobe software – the industry standard for multimedia work. Panic gripped me. Then, another thought surfaced:

When you need it, you will have it.

Swallowing hard, I dragged the software folder to the recycle bin. This time, it was even harder. But as I did, peace washed over me.

God was teaching me the blessing of obedience and trust in him in a real, tangible way.

How often do our 'small' acts of disobedience hold us back from moving forward in the things of God?

In my first three years as a Christian, this was painfully true. I had lied to staff at Teen Challenge, slept with an old girlfriend, started drinking again, and claimed benefits I wasn't entitled to. Each act grieved the Holy Spirit and hindered my growth.

Obedience to God's Word and the inner promptings of the Holy Spirit are foundational if we are to grow into the people God intends us to be. It's all part of what the Bible calls 'putting off the old man' and 'putting on the new'.[8]

And for those called to leadership, it's non-negotiable.

***

Upon completing the School of Ministry, I took on a six-month role at Teen Challenge as a support worker, eager to discern God's next steps for my life. I knew that before I could lead others, I had to first learn to serve under the leadership of those who had gone before me.

This was the model Jesus himself demonstrated – servant leadership. He didn't seek power or status; he humbled himself, washing the feet of his disciples, teaching that true leadership is rooted in service.[9] Too often, people desire to lead before they have learned to follow, but leadership without service breeds pride.

Serving first shaped my heart, deepened my dependence on God, and cultivated in me the qualities essential for any emerging leader – humility, a genuine love for others, and a willingness to be led. These lessons were far more valuable than any title or position I could ever attain.

***

8. Ephesians 4:22–24.
9. John 13:12–17.

Before I was ready for what lay ahead, God had one more lesson to teach me – one final step in breaking down my fear of failure and lack of self-belief.

'I hear you can build websites?' someone asked casually.

'Aye, that's right,' I replied.

'Would you build one for our charity?'

'I'd love to, but I don't have the software at the moment.'

'We'll buy it for you.'

'What?' I asked, caught completely off guard.

'Aye, as a charity, we get it at a fraction of the cost.'

'OK then! If you get me the software, I'll do it,' I said, a spark of excitement rising within me.

I could have played it safe with a WordPress template, but something inside me knew I had to build this one from scratch – designing and coding every element myself. It felt like more than just a project. It was a test. A divine opportunity to finally confront and overcome the fear of failure and the nagging self-doubt that had plagued me for years.

I was resolute: I will build this website from scratch. I can build this website from scratch.

One day, as I sat designing the layout using the brand-new Adobe software (the latest version, of course!), a thought stopped me mid-click: *Now you need the software . . . now you have it.*

It landed with quiet weight. I was instantly reminded of that earlier moment when I had dragged my pirated software into the recycle bin – trusting that small, faith-filled whisper: *You'll have it when you need it.*

And now here I was. I needed it. I had it.

The realisation deepened my faith even further. God had been teaching me to trust him not just in the big, spiritual moments, but in the everyday details. As I completed the site – code written, content aligned, design polished – I felt something shift. The voice of inadequacy went quiet. The fog of self-doubt lifted.

I was ready.

Ready to step into something completely unexpected . . .

One day, as I lay in my bedroom, a thought struck me with unexpected clarity:

I want you to start an outreach for King's Church.

I sat up, my heart pounding. *Me? Lead an outreach?* The familiar fear of failure crept in, but so did something else – a deepening trust in God. He had been steadily growing my faith, leading me through obedience checks, nudging me forward step by step. This first leadership call felt like a defining moment – a test of faith and willingness to move beyond my comfort zone.

I already knew Wales wasn't my long-term home, nor did I feel called to work for Teen Challenge indefinitely. My thoughts had been drifting back to London, to the church that had been my anchor during my first time there; the very people who had invested in me by funding my place at the School of Ministry. Launching an outreach for them felt like a natural next step.

As I wrestled with the idea, I was reminded of the first sermon I had been asked to preach during my ministry training. My passage was:

> 'Very truly I tell you, unless a grain of wheat falls to the ground and dies, it remains only a single seed. But if it dies, it produces many seeds.'
>
> *(John 12:24)*

I had related this scripture to my own journey. In my first three years as a Christian, I had been like that grain of wheat that refused to die – still living for myself, pursuing my own plans, asking God to bless my agenda instead of surrendering to his. But through the school of hard knocks, I had learned that true fruitfulness only comes through surrender.

And now, leadership was the place where this fruit would truly grow. But God knew something I didn't yet fully grasp – that I would need someone special in my life to help me carry the weight of what lay ahead . . .

Chapter 8

A Destined Partner

This is the woman I have for you. She will be your wife.

I sat back, stunned.

Did that really just happen? My mind raced as I tried to recreate the scene that had just flashed before my eyes.

A surge of excitement bubbled up inside me. *Thank you, Lord!* I wanted to shout, but I kept it to myself. Talking during evening class at Teen Challenge wasn't allowed, and the last thing I needed was a discipline slip.

I put down the book I had been reading, my thoughts spinning. The image had come and gone in the blink of an eye – a stunning girl I had never met before, her face vivid yet fleeting. It had caught me completely off guard.

I would later realise this was the fulfilment of a deep longing in my heart, from the dream during my first Teen Challenge programme. But this time, everything was different. I had surrendered fully, putting God first in all things. And this moment happened, sitting in the classroom during my second programme, which felt like God was confirming what was to come, giving me the smallest glimpse of the woman he had prepared for me.

Wow! She's beautiful. The thought settled warmly in my heart. I decided to keep this to myself, letting the moment sink in as I quietly waited for its fulfilment, having full assurance that God would bring this to pass in his perfect timing.

***

'Hi, my name's Julie. I'm twenty-seven years old and from a town called Erskine, on the outskirts of Glasgow.'

She's pretty, I thought to myself as I settled in to listen to her share her story at church.

'I recently read that the '80s were considered one of the most carefree eras, and for me, that was true. I grew up in a loving, stable family with my mum, dad, younger brother and sister. Everything was good.' She paused. 'I certainly can't blame my upbringing for the way my life turned out, as it spiralled out of control and into a life of addiction.'

Wow. You would never think she had been through addiction, I mused.

'I always believed in God. At school, we would sing songs about him during assembly, but my family had no real faith. My mum believed in God but didn't practise any religion. My dad was an atheist. My grandparents had conflicting beliefs – one a Jehovah's Witness, the other dismissing it all as nonsense. As I grew up, I saw the world in two parts: God's way and the devil's way. And I started being drawn to what the devil had to offer.'

She took a deep breath. 'By Primary 6, I was already going off the rails. I started smoking in Primary 7, and by the summer before high school, I was experimenting with alcohol.'

She started drinking earlier than I did. We all know where this is going, I thought grimly.

'My teenage years were pure chaos. I lived to get drunk. I was regularly suspended from school and eventually expelled at fourteen, never getting to sit my exams. By fifteen, I was drinking almost every day, drowning out depression, self-hatred, guilt and shame. I'd black out, wake up regretting everything. Then, at fifteen, I found out I was pregnant. My daughter Zoe was born a week before my sixteenth birthday. I quit drinking and smoking for a while, but soon after, I relapsed. By seventeen, I was pregnant again. My son Marc was born just before my eighteenth birthday.'

Her voice wavered slightly, but she pressed on.

'I tried to get my life together. I went to college, hoping for a fresh start. But one day, after class, I went to the pub with some students. That night, I ended up at a house party where I tried heroin for the first time. Soon after, Zoe and Marc were placed in foster care.'

She swallowed hard. 'Not only had I lost my kids, but I was addicted to heroin, hooked on Valium, and stuck on methadone – something I swore I'd never do. I hated it. Hated the way it made me feel. Hated being chained to the chemist, pretending methadone was the answer when I was still using anything else I could get my hands on.'

She paused, her voice softer now. 'One morning, after another sleepless night, I cried out to God: "If you help me, I promise to follow you all the days of my life." I was done. My mum had contacted a woman named June Ross, who helped me get into Teen Challenge. In June 2009, I entered Hope House.'

A small smile crossed her face. 'It was there I truly found faith. Jesus transformed my life. I'm no longer that broken woman. I have an amazing relationship with Zoe, Marc and my parents now. I'm so grateful to my mum and dad for stepping in and giving my kids the stability they needed. And I hope to move back soon – to be the mum they deserve.'

She took a deep breath. 'Thank you to the staff at Hope House who never gave up on me. I will be forever grateful.'

The room erupted in applause as she made her way back to her seat.

I clapped along, but my thoughts started to wander. *She's pretty . . . but not for me. I need someone from a different background. Someone who's not been in addiction. Someone brought up in a Christian home. Aye, that's what I need.*

I'd convinced myself that was the kind of woman I should marry.

But God had other plans. He knew exactly what he was doing – and just how significant this woman would become in my life.

***

'That was good tonight, wasn't it?' I said, my heart still buzzing from the evening.

'Yeah, we had some really great conversations,' Julie replied, her voice full of excitement. 'We make a pretty good team, don't we?'

'We certainly do,' I said with a smile, locking eyes with her. Those big, beautiful, emerald eyes – whoa. *She really is pretty,* I thought to myself.

A sudden wave of awkwardness passed between us. We both sensed it – this was more than just working together on outreach. Something deeper was stirring.

As if by some divine setup, we kept getting paired together for street outreach with a small evangelical church in Llanelli, South Wales. It was something we were both passionate about, but now, I was sensing a new passion bubbling up inside me – and it had nothing to do with outreach!

What is going on? I questioned myself as my heart began to race.

I can't . . . I shouldn't . . . She's also been . . . but I couldn't ignore this. My thoughts swirled as I stole another glance at her, forcing a small, nervous smile to break the silence. Not an awkward silence – more like an unspoken understanding, something neither of us could quite articulate yet.

I stopped in my tracks.

Julie turned to me, concern flickering across her face. 'You OK, Ricky?'

'Well . . .' I hesitated.

'What's up?' she asked, her voice softer now.

'Julie . . .'

'What?'

'Julie, I think . . .' My words trailed off as my pulse quickened.

'Think what?' she asked, tilting her head slightly.

The moment stretched between us, charged with something undeniable. As our eyes locked, something clicked – something neither of us could run from.

I leaned forward and kissed her.

Something special was unfolding. What I didn't know yet was that, for Julie, it had already begun long before this moment.

***

'So, you looking forward to moving back to Glasgow?' I asked, taking a slow sip of my latte.

Julie shifted in her seat, getting comfortable. 'Yes and no,' she said, her voice carrying a mix of excitement and hesitation.

'I can't wait to be back with Zoe and Marc, to be their mum again. But I'm going to miss my friends, the life I've built here in Wales over the past two years.' She paused, eyes dropping to her coffee cup.

'And . . . well–' she hesitated, clearly uncomfortable.

'Well, what?' I pressed, sensing there was more.

She glanced up at me, her big green eyes piercing straight through. 'You know. And you, of course.'

I felt a warmth spread through my chest. 'I know. Me too,' I admitted, the weight of her upcoming move suddenly feeling heavier.

We were sitting in a quaint little coffee shop in Ammanford, South Wales, having what would be our last proper sit-down before Julie left for Glasgow. The thought gnawed at me. The conversation lulled, the background chatter of the café filling the silence. Then, without fully thinking, I blurted out, 'Julie, do you feel you've heard from God about our relationship?'

She blinked. 'What?'

'Well . . .' I leaned in, sure I'd hit on something. 'You do, don't you?'

She exhaled, a small smirk forming. 'Maybe.'

I laughed, shaking my head. 'So when? How?'

Julie refocused, locking her gaze onto mine. Her tone shifted, serious now. 'Ricky, I want you to hear for yourself. You're going back to London in a few weeks, so why don't we take a month without contact – just seeking God, asking him to give you clarity about us?'

I paused, considering it. The idea of not speaking for a whole month felt daunting but, deep down, I knew it was right. It was classic Julie – her ability to bring wisdom into any situation, something I would come to recognise as one of her greatest strengths.

'Aye, OK. Let's do that,' I said, nodding.

She exhaled, a satisfied smile appearing. 'Good. Because it's important that you hear from God about us.'

The weight of the moment lingered between us, but soon, we eased back into our usual rhythm, chatting and laughing until it was time to go. Within weeks, Julie was back in Glasgow, and I was back in London.

Let the seeking begin.

***

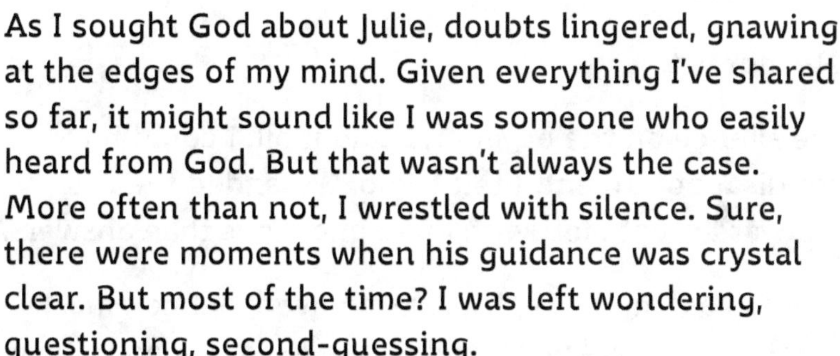

As I sought God about Julie, doubts lingered, gnawing at the edges of my mind. Given everything I've shared so far, it might sound like I was someone who easily heard from God. But that wasn't always the case. More often than not, I wrestled with silence. Sure, there were moments when his guidance was crystal clear. But most of the time? I was left wondering, questioning, second-guessing.

This was one of those times.

Weeks passed. I fasted. I prayed. I pleaded for direction. Yet still – nothing. The silence was deafening, and the deadline loomed. Soon, I'd be speaking to Julie again.

Panic crept in. I needed an answer.

***

In the back of my mind, I knew Julie believed she'd already heard from God about us. Instead of bringing peace, it only added pressure.

The day before we were due to speak, I sent her a simple message: 'Hi.'

Shortly after, as I lay on my bed, my phone rang. My heart pounded as I answered.

After a few minutes of small talk, she asked the question we'd both been waiting for.

'So, did you hear anything?'

The pause felt endless. I swallowed.

'No, not yet.'

The silence on the other end said it all. I could feel her disappointment. I felt it too. We ended the call awkwardly, both left with more questions than answers.

As soon as I hung up, frustration overwhelmed me. I dropped to my knees, crying out, 'God, I need to hear from you.'

The pressure was real. I only wanted God's will. Nothing more. Nothing less.

***

A few days later, the breakthrough came.

I don't remember how I ended up in 1 Timothy in the Bible, but as I read, two verses gripped me:

> 'I also want the women to dress modestly, with decency and propriety . . . but with good deeds, appropriate for women who profess to worship God.'
>
> *(1 Timothy 2:9–10)*

As I meditated, something clicked. These weren't just instructions – they were a picture. The kind of woman I'd been praying for. And in that moment, I saw Julie.

Humble. Godly. Loving. Not only outwardly beautiful but filled with a quiet strength.

I had been looking with the wrong eyes – worldly eyes. And now it was as if Scripture was saying, this is her.

Julie, Julie, Julie.

Waves of joy, certainty and peace swept through me. The memory of the classroom vision returned – her face so vivid, the words so clear: *This is the woman I have for you.*

I knew. I knew deep down – God had given the clarity I needed. Julie was the woman he had for me.

I grabbed my phone and dialled.

'Hello?'

'I've heard from God!' I blurted.

A breath caught on the other end. 'You have?'

I poured it all out – the verse, the vision, the peace. Every detail. As I spoke, certainty grew.

And in my heart, I knew what had to come next.

Julie's birthday was just around the corner. I bought the ring. I was going to propose.

***

On a beautiful London summer evening, the city was bathed in golden light – perfect for what was about to unfold. I arrived at the house of one of our church elders where Julie was staying, nerves bubbling under the surface.

'Riiiicckkkyyy!' he called excitedly as I stepped inside. 'Wait till you see Julie!' He grinned, waving me through to the garden.

Then I saw her.

'Wow . . .' The word escaped before I could stop it. Julie stood in a yellow summer dress, sunlight catching her big green eyes and radiant smile.

'You look stunning,' I said, heart thudding.

She laughed softly, her cheeks flushed. 'Let's make this a birthday to remember,' I said as we walked to the front door.

'Hold on – let me get a photo of the fantastic couple.' A quick snap, a knowing wink from the elder. The plan was in motion.

We wandered through Valentines Park, the air filled with birdsong and laughter. But despite the perfect setting, my nerves were intensifying.

After taking the Tube into the heart of the West End, Julie turned to me, curious. 'So . . . where are we going?'

I smirked. 'All in good time.'

I barely remember the Indian meal beforehand – my stomach was too knotted with nerves. Julie caught on quickly.

'Are you OK, Ricky? You're not quite yourself tonight.'

'Aye, I'm good,' I said, forcing a smile. 'You're going to love what's next.'

We settled into our seats at the theatre for *Phantom of the Opera*. As the music swelled, so did my nerves. Julie sensed it.

'Why does he look so nervous?' she later recalled thinking. *'He's usually so calm and collected.'*

At the end of the show, I leaned over, still clapping. 'That was amazing, wasn't it?'

'It sure was,' she smiled. 'Thanks for making this such a special birthday.' She kissed my cheek.

Leaving the theatre, I hailed a rickshaw. 'To the Thames, please.'

As we zipped through the city lights, Julie's hand found mine, her head resting on my shoulder. I wrapped my arm around her, heart pounding.

'Let's stop here,' I told the rider. From here, it was a short walk along the River Thames to St Paul's Cathedral – my chosen spot.

As we crossed Millennium Bridge, I imagined a quiet, cinematic moment . . . but it was packed. Classic Central London.

Trying to stay composed, I gestured to the skyline. 'Look at that view – Tower Bridge lit up, and St Paul's looks amazing.'

'It really is,' she agreed, taking it in.

No more waiting.

I took a deep breath, dropped to one knee, and pulled the ring from my pocket. Her eyes widened as I looked up.

'Julie,' I said, my voice shaking slightly, 'will you marry me?'

For a moment, the world fell silent. A small crowd had gathered.

'Yes, I will,' she said softly, emotion in her voice.

As I slipped the ring on her finger and stood to hug her, the crowd erupted into applause.

Years later, Julie would laugh about that night. 'I really thought you were such a romantic! You set the bar so high – and have struggled to live up to it!'

I always grinned and replied, 'Aye, but it worked, didn't it?'

And while I might not always reach those dizzy heights, I do try to recreate such romanticism from time to time.

***

Over the next few months, we saw God lead and provide in ways that deeply strengthened our faith.

The first big question was: where should we live – London or Glasgow?

On the surface, London seemed the obvious choice. I had a good job using my multimedia qualifications, was serving with Teen Challenge London, and had launched the outreach café in Ilford, which was already bearing fruit. But as we prayed and talked it through, both of us sensed a strong pull towards Glasgow. It wasn't the choice I'd expected – or even wanted, if I'm honest. Glasgow had a reputation for being tough, known for high levels of poverty, crime and violence. But I was learning that a surrendered life means trusting God's direction over my own preferences. Zoe and Marc were already settled in school there, and God knew what lay ahead.

Julie and I had always said there was no point dragging things out. We set our wedding date for 2nd February 2013 – just two days before my thirty-fourth birthday. That gave us under six months to prepare. We didn't have much money, but again and again, God provided. Weddings can cost a fortune, but through the generosity of friends who stepped in to help, we managed to pull off a beautiful day for a fraction of the usual cost. We remain deeply grateful for every act of kindness that made it possible.

As I prepared to relocate, my biggest concern was leaving King's Café. I didn't want to let the church down, especially after putting so much heart into launching the outreach. But once again, God had it covered. A brilliant couple, along with a friend who'd supported the café from day one, stepped up to lead the work. To this day, they continue to serve the homeless community in Ilford, and the outreach is still going strong.

Our wedding day was everything we'd hoped for. Everything ran like clockwork, and as we stood hand in hand, we knew this was just the beginning. A new chapter. A new adventure. One we were ready to embrace – together.

***

'Ricky, I don't know what to do.'

'What's wrong?' I asked, swivelling round in my chair, pausing from my work to give Julie my full attention.

'My friend has pulled out,' she said anxiously, pacing the room. 'She's got too much on her plate and can't commit to starting a ministry for women on the streets of Glasgow.' Her voice wavered. 'You know how much this has been on my heart. What am I going to do? I can't do this on my own . . .'

'OK, when's the meeting with the church to discuss your idea?' I asked, trying to calm her down.

'In two days,' she replied, flustered. 'I can't—'

I quickly cut in, 'I'll come with you. I'll support you.'

'Will you?' she said, her expression shifting from anxiety to relief. 'Will you really?' She sounded surprised. 'I thought you wanted a break from ministry for a while?'

'I do,' I admitted, 'but I want to be there for you as you present your idea to the church leadership.'

She threw her arms around me. 'Oh, Ricky, that means so much to me! You're going to love Peter,' she added, excitement returning to her voice. 'He's such a visionary leader.'

Little did I know just how significant the merging of our paths would prove to be.

Chapter 9

Birthing of a Ministry

'When you're in your church building, the doors are open and the lights are on – but the city is virtually empty. When the people are in the city, your building is closed, in darkness, and locked up. REVERSE THAT!'

Peter's strong Welsh accent rang out as he waved his hands, eyes gleaming with passion.

'That's what I heard the Lord say to me – simple and clear, but it was such a stimulating moment because, boy, did I need to hear this!'

He leaned forward, his tone shifting to quiet reflection.

'I'd arrived in Glasgow in September 2000 after many fruitful years leading a growing church in Bradford. But I came under a dark, heavy cloud. A denominational issue had crushed my wife and me. And then I stepped into a large city centre church with a small, ageing congregation clattering around in it. It was bleak.'

He paused, his face heavy with memory.

'Then on Monday, 16th October, I found myself on my knees. I was crying out to God. That's when I heard those words. And right there – faith rose in my heart. Hope and energy returned. I was filled with a newfound excitement and enthusiasm.'

Peter was a larger-than-life character. Visionary, energising, and empowering – his leadership had a way of drawing you in. He carried a father's heart and the kind of spiritual authority that inspired others to believe bigger, dream deeper, and step forward in faith.

He pointed to the wall.

'The mission statement of the church at the time was "Bringing the healing love of God to a hurting world". That's exactly what we're doing through the outreach now. Seeing it fulfilled after all these years – it moves me, Ricky. It really does.'

His eyes welled up, emotion catching in his voice.

'So, how did you meet Julie then?' I asked, intrigued, as we looked out the window towards the City Chambers and George Square.

Peter sat back, his grin returning.

'Well, we were running a very successful café called Café Connect. It was so busy that queues ran through the café, out into the foyer, even onto the street! But my heart longed for more than a social space – I wanted a ministry with real gospel impact.

'Then, one day, I got a call from Pastor John Macey at Teen Challenge UK. "Peter," he said, "do you know anyone in Glasgow who could house a young woman returning from our women's rehab programme? Her name's Julie."

'As soon as I put the phone down, something stirred in my spirit. I couldn't explain it. I just knew God was in it.'

He smiled.

'Julie joined the café team and began attending church. And not long after, I heard about you. Your path, her path, ours – all converging. Only God could orchestrate something like that.'

***

We launched Café Connect on Saturday, 4th May 2013. Friday nights already had other Christian outreaches running in the city, but Saturdays were wide open. We didn't want to duplicate efforts – we wanted to fill a gap.

In the lead-up, Julie and I rallied support from our church and beyond. Around thirty to forty people turned up that evening. I wasn't sure they all knew what they were in for!

We arrived at 7 p.m. to set up, and by 7:30, the room was buzzing with chatter and expectancy.

'OK everyone, can I have your attention?' I called out, raising my voice above the noise.

The room quieted, and I continued, 'Thanks for coming along to the first night of Café Connect outreach!' Smiles were exchanged, eyes full of curiosity and anticipation.

'But here's the thing,' I said, pausing to build suspense. 'No one knows we're here yet. So, let me tell you what we're going to do tonight.'

I noticed some faces shifting from excitement to mild confusion as I explained.

'A small team will stay back here in the café, but the rest of us will hit the streets in teams of two or three. We've printed some flyers with the café's location and opening times. Grab a bundle, and let's get out there!'

Off we went. That first evening, we made countless connections on the streets – and a handful of folks came back with us.

It was official. The ministry had begun.

From my previous experience of starting a similar outreach in Ilford, I knew the truth of this scripture:

> 'Do not despise these small beginnings, for the LORD rejoices to see the work begin.'
>
> *(Zechariah 4:10 NLT)*

Little did I know, an unexpected phone call was coming the next day . . .

***

'Hello, Ricky, Peter here.'

'Hi, Peter, how are you?'

'Well, you see, two of the men who came back to the café last night also came along to church today.'

'Fantastic! Praise God!' I replied, not fully picking up on the tone in which Peter had broken the news.

After a brief pause, Peter continued, more hesitantly. 'Well, yes, it's great they came, but an incident occurred after the service.'

'Oh, I see,' I said, now slightly concerned. 'What happened?'

'As you know from your recent visits, we congregate in the café after the service for tea, coffee and fellowship.'

'Uh-huh,' I replied.

'One of the men tried to walk out the front door with a handbag under his jacket, but thankfully one of the stewards was on hand. He saw the man heading towards the door with a massive bulge in his jacket and stopped him, asking, "What's that in your jacket?"

'The man replied, "What you on aboot?" then turned back, rushed into the café to put the handbag back, and slipped out the side door.'

'Oh no, I'm really sorry to hear that, Peter,' I said. 'So nothing was taken?'

'No, thankfully. But it's given us a bit of a shake-up. We're not used to having homeless or addicted people in our services.'

As the call ended, I lowered the phone and turned to Julie, still processing what I'd just heard.

'Maybe we need to go to the church for a while – help them get used to this transition?' I said, my voice laced with both concern and a growing sense of responsibility.

Julie paused for a moment, thinking it over, before nodding. 'Yes, we should.'

Without hesitation, I picked up the phone and called Peter back.

'Peter, Julie and I have been talking, and we think it would be good for us to come along to the church for a while – to help everyone get used to things,' I said.

There was a brief silence, then an unmistakable burst of enthusiasm came through the receiver.

'Marvellous! Absolutely marvellous!' Peter exclaimed in that rich Welsh accent of his, his excitement practically vibrating down the line. 'This is wonderful news!'

I must point out here that both Julie and I had originally planned to help the church get the outreach up and running, supporting it for a few months before moving to a church in our local community in Govan, Glasgow. We'd intended to hand over leadership of the outreach to someone in the congregation at Glasgow City Church, just as I'd done previously in Ilford.

We knew God had called us to Govan and hoped to do our ministry there while being part of a local fellowship.

But as it says in the Bible, 'In their hearts humans plan their course, but the LORD establishes their steps' (Proverbs 16:9).

The Lord had other ideas. His vision for our lives – and this work – was far greater than we could have imagined.

At first, all we wanted was to reach out to those on the streets of Glasgow city centre – people struggling with addiction and the chaos it brings – and hopefully see some come to know Jesus, and experience the same life transformation we had experienced.

But God also has his timing and his ways. Our job is to follow where he leads.

We would go on to spend eight years at Glasgow City Church before God opened the door for us to be part of a church in our local community.

***

After the buzz of that first night, reality hit us hard the following Saturday. The excitement had worn off, and instead of the thirty to forty volunteers we'd had initially, we were down to around eight – including Julie and me.

I glanced around the room as the clock ticked towards 8 p.m., the once-crowded space now looking a little too spacious.

'Well,' I said, exhaling slowly, 'looks like we've got our core team.'

Julie gave me a knowing smile. 'I think people expected something different,' she said, leaning against the counter.

I nodded. It was clear now – some had thought this would be a structured outreach, the kind where they could sit comfortably, 'being blessed', listen to worship, hear a testimony, and be inspired by an evangelistic message. But this wasn't about being comfortable. It was about being a blessing. It was about stepping out, meeting people where they were, and offering them practical help, real conversation, and a bit of hope.

And not everyone was up for that.

As the weeks passed, our numbers fluctuated. But something encouraging happened – our core team solidified. Those who remained were committed. Some came every week, some monthly, and others whenever they could. But we always had enough – enough to run the café, enough to send teams onto the streets, enough to keep showing up, rain or shine.

One evening, as Julie and I unlocked the doors, I noticed something different.

'Julie, look,' I said, nodding towards the street.

A small group of people stood waiting outside, hands in pockets, huddled against the cold.

She smiled. 'They know we're here for them.'

Word had spread. The café was no longer just a place we ran – it was becoming a place people relied on.

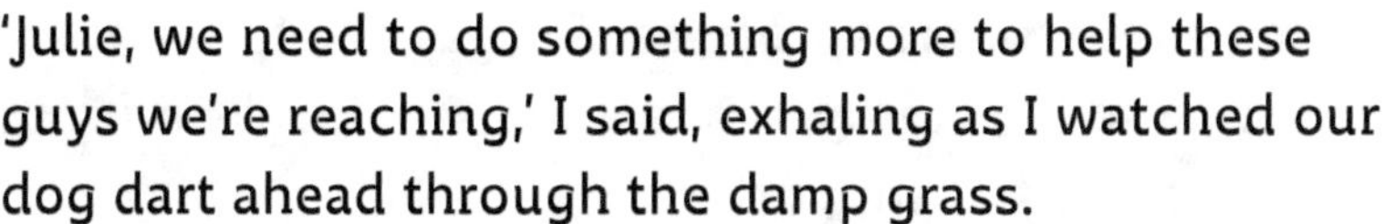

'Julie, we need to do something more to help these guys we're reaching,' I said, exhaling as I watched our dog dart ahead through the damp grass.

Julie glanced at me, intrigued. 'What are you thinking, Ricky?'

As we strolled through the local park in Govan, the weight of the thought pressed more heavily on me. 'It's brilliant that we're connecting with so many people on the streets and seeing them come into the drop-in café. Some are even making it to church on Sundays.' I paused. 'But what about the rest of the week?'

Julie nodded, her expression shifting to one of excitement. 'I know exactly what you mean! But isn't it incredible how some of these men are finding faith?'

'Aye, it's amazing.' I grinned, feeling the joy of what we were witnessing. 'But I don't just want them to find faith, Julie.' Stopping in my tracks, I turned to look her straight in the eye. 'I want them to break free from their addictions. I need to do something more.'

She paused for a moment, her brow furrowing. 'But you're working full-time during the week–'

Before she could say another word, I jumped in. 'Exactly! That's why I'm thinking about taking a couple of afternoons off work to meet with these guys one-to-one. Help them take those next steps, prepare them for rehab.'

A huge smile spread across her face as she flung her arms around me. 'Ricky, that's a brilliant idea! Go for it! You've got my full support.'

I hugged her back, feeling a fresh wave of purpose surge through me. This was the next step. The work wasn't just about getting people through the door – it was about helping them find a way out.

In the early days of our outreach, the model we used – street outreach, a drop-in café, one-to-one support, and rehab referrals – quickly became the heartbeat of our service. We began seeing the first glimmers of transformation, the kind of change that would fuel our hope and shape the journey ahead.

One evening stands out as a powerful example of how simple acts of love and consistency can lead to life-altering breakthroughs.

It was a busy Saturday night, and we were out in Glasgow's city centre. Amid the buzz of nightlife, we noticed a man sitting on the pavement near a cash machine – a common spot for begging, nestled between pubs and takeaway shops.

We introduced ourselves, but he wasn't particularly keen to talk. I handed him a flyer for the café and said gently, 'You're welcome to come by any time.' He shook his head. Still, I pressed in slightly, asking about his situation. Eventually, he shared that he was staying in homeless accommodation nearby and was battling heroin and street Valium addiction.

Before we left, I asked, 'Would it be OK if we prayed for you?'

A reluctant, 'Aye, alright,' was his reply.

We prayed there and then – a simple prayer asking for God's blessing, strength, and freedom. Then we left, not knowing if we'd ever see him again.

Later, we found out what happened next. The following morning, Roger woke up feeling angry and unsettled. As he later shared with us, the experience of being prayed for lingered. 'Who do they think they are, praying for me?' he muttered. But the encounter stayed with him. He couldn't shake it. Over the days that followed, the memory kept resurfacing – the conversation, the kindness, the prayer.

In the weeks that followed, we crossed paths again during outreach. Slowly, his resistance began to soften. One Saturday night, we invited him to the café again – and to our surprise, he said yes.

From that night on, he became a regular. Saturday evenings at the café became a small refuge. Then came Sundays. He started attending church, blending into the crowd at the back. With each week, something began to shift.

He told us: 'In the café, I felt something I hadn't felt in years – love. I felt accepted. I couldn't even remember the last time anyone made me feel like that.'

Then one Sunday, during a particularly moving time of worship, Roger experienced a turning point.

'Up at the back of the church,' he told us later, 'I said a prayer to become a Christian . . . in a ball of snot and tears.'

From there, our relationship deepened. We started meeting one-to-one, and he told me he wanted to go to rehab. After months of encouragement and support, we helped him take the steps needed to enter a programme.

There, he detoxed from methadone and other substances. For the first time in years, he was clean.

Roger's journey wasn't easy, but it was real. His story remains a powerful example of what God can do when we simply show up, offer love, and trust him with the results. It's proof that no matter how rough the road, transformation is always possible – one step at a time.

***

'Peter, this thought keeps coming to me, "It's time to step into full-time ministry," and I feel like I need to act on it,' I said, my voice heavy with both excitement and uncertainty.

Peter looked at me, his expression thoughtful. 'Sounds like the Lord's leading, Ricky.'

I nodded. 'That's what I think too, but I've got a family to take care of, and I'm the main provider . . .' My voice trailed off, the weight of responsibility pressing on my chest.

Peter's eyes locked onto mine, full of assurance. 'If the Lord is in it,' he began, his voice steady, 'he'll make a way.'

I took a deep breath, trying to settle my thoughts. 'Aye, I've already been thinking about that. I've spoken to a couple of people about how I could raise funds to cover the shortfall.'

Peter nodded, his attention fully on me. 'Uh-huh.' He leaned in, eager for the next part.

'Well,' I began, 'I was thinking of starting with three full days in ministry and continuing to work self-employed on my computer for two days. A progressive step of faith, if that makes sense?'

Peter's face softened with understanding. 'Yes, that makes perfect sense . . .' His voice trailed off, as if he could see the road ahead more clearly than I could.

With a burst of enthusiasm, I couldn't help but interject. 'I plan to speak at a few churches I've been connected with, asking people to sponsor me. So, do you think I could ask for support at our church?'

Peter's face lit up, and I could see the excitement in his eyes. 'Absolutely, Ricky! I'm sure the church would be behind you, and I'll speak to the leadership team about helping with the funding too.'

I felt a surge of hope, and not long after, I had the opportunity to speak at two other churches. To my amazement, it wasn't long before I had raised enough support to bring me close to what I was earning before. God's faithfulness was undeniable, and by the beginning of 2014, I was ready to fully step into the ministry.

As I looked back, I realised another theme was beginning to emerge in my journey: the importance of taking steps of faith. This would become a constant in my life, as God's call to trust him more grew stronger every day.

One day, as we sat in Peter's office during one of our regular catch-ups, he said something that took me by surprise. 'Ricky, I think we need to set this work up as its own charity.'

I blinked, taken aback. 'What? A charity?'

Peter nodded confidently. 'Yes. We're seeing so much fruit already. If we stay just an outreach of the church, we're going to limit its potential.'

I didn't know what was involved, but deep down, I knew he was right. I replied without hesitation, 'Let's do it.'

Peter smiled, his eyes gleaming. 'Praise God! I don't think I've told you this before, but I live by this mantra: "I would rather attempt to do something big for Jesus and fail, than attempt to do nothing and succeed."

And this work, Ricky, fits perfectly with that. So do you and Julie.'

Years later, I learned something that made that moment even more significant. When Peter had been a pastor in Bradford, he'd played a key role in establishing Transforming Lives for Good (TLG)[10] as a charity. What had started as a youth outreach in his church had grown into a national charity working with churches to support young people in need. I believe his experience with TLG deeply influenced his vision for our work and gave him a passion to see it grow.

Before we could submit our application for charity status, there was one final thing to decide: the name. We wanted something that reflected our mission of connecting with people, and that also tied back to the café outreach we had started.

After brainstorming together, we chose the name: Street Connect.

On 23rd May 2014, just over a year after we had begun as a small church outreach, we received confirmation of our registered charity status.

It was becoming clear God was beginning to do something special – and that I might well be here longer than originally anticipated!

10. Transforming Lives for Good (TLG) – Official website: *About Us* https://www.tlg.org.uk/about-tlg (accessed August 2025).

Chapter 10

Trials and Temptations

'Ricky! Ricky!' the voice rang out, each call more aggressive, more venomous. Fists pounded the door with increasing force. 'I know you're in there! Open the door!' His breathing was heavy, ragged with fury.

I looked across the room. My colleague was clearly shaken, her face pale with fear.

Then his voice dropped to a menacing growl. 'I know where you live, and you better watch your back when you're out on the streets. Because I'll be watching.'

Silence.

My heart thudded in my chest. *Has he gone?*

'Do you think he's left?' she whispered, her voice barely steady.

I exhaled slowly. 'I think so. Are you alright?'

She nodded hesitantly. 'Yeah . . . I think so.' Then, after a pause, 'Are we still going out on the streets today? After what he just said?'

I hesitated, weighing the risk. 'Maybe best to leave it for today,' I admitted. 'But I'm not going to let him stop us doing this work. We'll get back out there in a few days – once things have settled.'

'Alright,' she murmured, still visibly shaken.

She was fresh out of university – just completed her Community Development degree at university – our second part-time team member at Street Connect, after myself. Eager, full of hope, but new to the harsh realities of frontline ministry.

'Let's focus on those funding applications for now,' I said, offering some direction.

But my thoughts were spinning. I replayed *his* story in my head. He'd been homeless when we met – just out of prison, feared on the streets. Raised in one of Glasgow's toughest neighbourhoods, his life had been steeped in violence, gangs, and guns. He'd spent most of his adult life in and out of prison.

But we'd connected. He'd engaged with everything we offered – our support services, church, even two rehab attempts. But each time, he left rehab early after falling out with staff and landed back on the streets.

Still, we hadn't given up on him. We knew how deep the pain went.

Things began to unravel when another church member reopened the church café to the public and offered him a volunteer role. It seemed positive at first. But he quickly began overstepping – gaining a set of keys, wandering the building like he owned it, interrupting private meetings, even barging into my office while I was with other service participants. It had to stop.

When I confronted him, something changed. His whole demeanour turned cold. And then came the threats.

So now here he was, outside the church, shouting up at my office window. And suddenly I knew – this wasn't just *him*. This was spiritual opposition. Street Connect was still fragile, barely taking root. And already, the devil was trying to choke it before it could grow.

We wrestle not against flesh and blood, I thought, recalling a Bible passage, *but against principalities and powers, spiritual forces of evil in the heavenly realms.*[11]

Fear whispered, *What if he does it? What if he catches me off guard one day on outreach? What if he does know where I live and comes to my house?*

I stared out the window, my fists clenched. I could feel the cold shadow of fear creeping in. But then another thought came to mind – quiet, firm, familiar.

11. Ephesians 6:12.

'Do not fear, for I am with you' (Isaiah 41:10).

I stood up slowly. *'Lord,'* I prayed silently, *'I don't want to live in fear. This work is yours. I trust you to protect it. And to protect us.'* I felt strength rise up within me. A resilience. I will not back down.

We prayed as a team. We trod carefully, but never once encountered him on the streets during that season.

That is – until one unforgettable Saturday night.

'Which volunteers are coming tonight?' Julie asked as we prepared the café for outreach.

'We've got Cr—'

BANG!

The sudden noise made Julie jump. 'What was that?' she gasped.

Before I could answer, we heard heavy footsteps pounding up the café stairs.

And then – *he* appeared.

He stood in the doorway, eyes blazing. 'So, Ricky. I've finally caught up wae ye.'

Julie stepped forward quickly. 'Look, you know you're banned. We don't want any trouble. Just leave.'

His head snapped towards her. 'You, shut yer mouth! It's HIM I'm after!' He took a step closer. 'Nobody here to help you now, is there?'

His voice rose in anger, spilling obscenities. Then, in one surreal moment, he grabbed a large, one-metre statue of a dog – one he had somehow brought into the café weeks earlier – and lifted it above his head.

'Now you're gettin' it!' he shouted, charging forward.

Time froze.

And then, something rose up in me – something I didn't plan, didn't think about. The words flew from my mouth: 'In the name of Jesus, I command you to put that down!'

The air shifted.

His body stopped mid-motion. His expression faltered. Eyes flickering, unsure. Slowly, he lowered the statue, his feet retreating.

'In the name of Jesus?' he muttered, disoriented. 'What you on aboot?'

Then he turned and walked out.

Silence.

I exhaled sharply, adrenaline still pulsing. The power in Jesus' name – it was real. Undeniable.

In that moment, I saw the true battle wasn't against John. It was against something much deeper, much darker.

But the fight wasn't quite over.

The following Saturday, as we locked up and headed for the car, I stopped abruptly. Both wing mirrors on our car had been smashed clean off.

Julie gasped. 'Ricky . . .'

I glared at the damage. 'It's him. It has to be.'

Anger surged in my chest. Fists clenched, I was raging. But I held it in.

We drove home in silence, the broken mirrors clacking against the doors. Halfway through the journey, Julie spoke.

'Consider it pure joy, my brothers and sisters, whenever you face trials of many kinds.'[12]

I shot her a look. 'Not now, Julie.'

Talk about poorly timed scripture sharing.

Still . . . she was right.

Eventually, the storm passed. He landed back in prison. And when he reappeared, it was as if none of it had ever happened. He no longer asked for our help. Occasionally he'd pop in, leave a message. But the threats stopped.

We have a principle at Street Connect: we don't give up on people. But we do protect our team. Sometimes,

12. James 1:2.

we have to put in boundaries. And if someone's willing to face their behaviour, we welcome them back.

Some return. Some don't.

It's worth noting that this was the only time I've ever handled a situation this way, and I've never encountered such strong opposition from a participant in our services since. This was clearly a one-time battle. A battle set to try and destroy the work of Street Connect.

But it didn't work.

The mission held.

And the work went on.

***

'So, what's your biggest challenge at the moment, Ricky?' asked Mark, one of my mentors, leaning forward with genuine curiosity as we sat in my office during one of our monthly sessions.

I let out a chuckle, shaking my head. 'Where do I even begin?' I sighed. 'I feel like I'm truly living the phrase: "Jack of all trades, master of none." Every day it's something new, and I'm learning everything on the job!'

Mark nodded knowingly. 'I know exactly how you feel, Ricky. I had to go through the same thing in the early days of planting the church.'

Sensing he really understood, I continued, 'Aye, I'm having to navigate working with the Board of Trustees, learning leadership and management, administration, project oversight, fundraising, running all the support services – and more!' I exhaled deeply, overwhelmed just listing it all.

Mark smiled, his voice steady and reassuring. 'This is invaluable experience, Ricky. Everything you're learning now will prepare you for what's ahead.'

I let his words sink in and nodded. 'Aye, I suppose you're right,' I admitted, feeling a little lighter.

Mark had a wealth of experience in urban ministry and leadership, having planted a church in one of the toughest areas in Glasgow. We had first met at a missions' conference in Manchester two years earlier, while I was still in London. After swapping contact details, we reconnected when I moved to Glasgow. Now, with the support of both Peter and Mark, I had two incredible leaders and mentors helping me navigate these uncharted waters.

***

'Ricky, I have someone I think you should connect with,' Mark said, his tone firm with conviction.

Intrigued, I leaned in. 'Oh? Who's that?'

'She's a manager at Bethany Christian Trust.[13] Have you heard of them?'

13. Bethany Christian Trust – Official website: *About Us* https://www.bethanychristiantrust.com/about-us/ (accessed August 2025).

'Aye, I have.' I replied, curiosity stirring.

'I think she – and Bethany – could be a great support to you,' he said.

'Brilliant. Can you put us in touch? We could use all the help we can get!'

And just like that, the connection was made. I quickly realised, she was the kind of leader who made things happen. Before long, we'd established a formal partnership, and soon after, Bethany employed me one day a week to lead our joint work.

It was a game-changer.

That extra day allowed me to step up to four days a week in ministry, edging me closer to my dream of going full-time. But it wasn't just about the hours; it was what they brought to the table. Bethany became a massive blessing to us; I often felt like we were receiving far more than we gave. They shared resources, provided guidance, and helped shape the way we operated.

I often found myself watching how they worked and thinking, *This is what I want Street Connect to become. Not a copy – but a ministry with strong values, strong systems, and strong impact.*

It was through that partnership that we introduced another vital service: Recovery Groups. Until then, we hadn't had the numbers or consistency to run group support. But momentum was building. We were also meeting more people who, for various reasons, weren't able – or willing – to go into residential rehab. We needed something local. Something that offered support in the community.

Bethany's Bridge to Freedom programme became the answer. We piloted it – and it worked. Soon after, we added another essential service: Aftercare Support. Men were returning from rehab, looking for guidance and community. Slowly but surely, all six pillars of our work were now in place.

That's when the unexpected conversation came.

During one of our regular supervision sessions, she leaned forward, her voice warm but serious.

'Ricky, I'm so encouraged by all that's happening through Street Connect.'

'Thanks,' I smiled. 'I am too.'

She paused, choosing her words carefully. 'Do you remember I mentioned I started a charity a few years back?'

'Aye, I remember.'

'But did you know I eventually merged it with Bethany?'

'Aye, Mark mentioned that.'

A knowing look crossed her face. 'Looking back, it was definitely the right decision. I've never once regretted it.'

I nodded, sensing there was more.

'I've been thinking . . . would you ever consider merging Street Connect with Bethany?'

The words hit like a jolt. I blinked, caught off guard. 'Eh . . . that's a big one. I'd need time to think. Pray. Speak to the Board – and to Julie, of course.'

'Of course,' she said gently. 'No pressure at all, Ricky. I just thought it could provide for you what it did for me – greater security, stability, and resources for the work you're already doing.'

And she was right. The offer was incredibly tempting. It would have given us a strong foundation, financial security, and the backing of a respected Christian organisation with more than 200 staff across Scotland.

For days, it played on my mind. The thought of stepping into something bigger, something more secure. I imagined the weight that would lift from my shoulders – no more wrestling over funding applications, no more uncertainty hanging over our future. It seemed like the obvious answer.

But as I sat with it, prayed about it, and talked it over with Julie and the Board, something inside me wouldn't settle.

This wasn't how the story was meant to go.

God had birthed this work. He had breathed life into it in a way no one else could. It was his vision, not mine. And I sensed, deep down, that joining another organisation – even one as excellent as Bethany – would mean handing over something God had entrusted us to shape.

Street Connect needed to stand on its own two feet. Not because we had something to prove, but because we had something unique to steward.

After much thought, discussion and prayer, I knew in my heart I had to say no.

I wasn't entirely sure what lay ahead. But I was certain of this: God had started something for a reason, and I was willing to trust his leading – wherever it took us next.

***

The offer to merge with Bethany stirred something deeper in me. It wasn't the first time I'd been tempted by a seemingly safer path – one that promised stability but threatened to pull me away from what I knew God had called me to.

I thought back to a conversation with one of the elders at church.

'Have you seen this job vacancy, Ricky? It would be perfect for you,' he said, handing me his phone.

I glanced at the screen. 'Looks interesting. I'll take a look,' I replied, not sure why he was bringing it up.

He hesitated, then gestured gently towards Julie's bump.

'With your growing family, maybe it's time to think about something more secure – something that offers stability for you and Julie.'

Something in me tightened. 'What do you mean?'

'You've had to raise your own support and, let's be honest, Street Connect is still pretty fragile.'

I forced a smile, pushing down the frustration rising in my chest. 'I'll pray about it, speak to Julie, and see where God leads.'

After they left, I closed the door and turned to Julie. 'He means well, and this would offer us security, but I really believe God's doing something special through Street Connect.'

She smiled, resting her hands on her growing bump. We already had two teenagers at home, and the reality of adding a newborn into the mix was beginning to hit.

'I feel the same,' she said. 'This isn't about comfort – it's about calling.'

'I'll take a proper look at it,' I said, 'but, deep down, I think I already know the answer.'

She nodded. 'Me too.'

I would have been a strong candidate. It paid more than I was making, and it came with structure, stability, and benefits. But it wasn't what we were called to. I knew that. So did Julie.

'This reminds me of when we first shared that we felt led to move to Govan and start the charity. Not everyone saw it – but we knew it was God.'

'We always seek wise counsel,' she said, 'but if their advice doesn't line up with what we sense God saying . . .'

'Then we follow God,' I said, the conviction settling in.

A few months later, our son was born. The following year, we welcomed our daughter. Life became beautifully chaotic: two teenagers, two in nappies, a hyper Jack Russell, and one more baby of sorts – the ever-growing work of Street Connect.

***

We had made incredible progress over the past year. At the start of 2015, we received our largest grant to date – enough to finally take me to five days a week. After a year of hustling, sacrificing, and trusting, my move to full-time had arrived.

Ironically, the moment I decided to stop my multimedia work, the website requests started flooding in. *Where were you all when I actually needed you?* I thought, shaking my head. I took on the first couple of projects, but it quickly became clear that I had to make a choice.

One evening, sitting at my desk, I sighed and closed my laptop. Julie walked in, sensing my hesitation.

'What's wrong?'

I exhaled. 'It's these website jobs. Now that I don't need them, they won't stop coming.'

She smiled knowingly. 'And?'

'And . . . I need to let them go. Fully. It's time to give everything to Street Connect,' I said, this time with conviction.

Julie leaned against the door frame, arms crossed. 'You already knew that, didn't you?'

I smirked. 'Aye, I suppose I did.'

Finally, being full-time – and on a full salary – felt surreal. Some days, I had to pinch myself. I'd sit back, letting it sink in, thinking, *Should I really be getting paid for this? For doing something I love? Something I'd do for free?*

The joy of marrying my vocation with my passion filled me with such gratitude. Every morning, I woke up with a sense of purpose in my heart.

I was living the dream.

Chapter 11

Shifting Sands

'Peter, the phrase "empowering the local church to reach the lost" keeps coming to mind,' I said during one of our monthly catch-ups in his small office at the top of the church.

Peter leaned back in his chair, tapping his fingers thoughtfully on the desk. 'Hmm . . . that's interesting. What do you think God's saying through it?'

I exhaled, feeling a spark of excitement. 'Well, now that we've clarified our service model with the six core services, and seen how fruitful it's been here in Glasgow city centre, I keep wondering – couldn't we replicate it in other parts of the city?'

Peter's eyes lit up. 'Go on . . . any areas in mind?'

I gave a short laugh. 'As you know, Peter, Glasgow's full of communities crying out for hope. And most already have churches at their heart. Why not partner with them? Equip them to reach people struggling with addiction using the same model we've been developing here?'

He leaned forward, his enthusiasm matching mine. 'Absolutely! I can really see the Lord's hand in this.'

'Me too. It's super exciting – yet, so unexpected,' I said, shaking my head. 'We only ever planned to launch a café outreach for the church and now here we are – a charity with a growing staff team, considering expansion across the city.'

Peter chuckled. 'Yes! The Lord is good and leads us on when we're faithful. Which actually brings me to something else I wanted to chat to you about.'

'Oh?' I said, intrigued.

'Well, you know I'm retiring as pastor this summer.'

I nodded. 'Aye.'

'And you know Alistair Matheson is taking over?'

'I've met him a few times now – really looking forward to getting to know him better.'

Peter smiled. 'Well, you certainly will. Ricky, you know how close Street Connect is to my heart.'

'I do, Peter.'

'I still plan to be on the Board of Trustees after I retire,' he said, then paused. 'But I think the senior leader of the church should serve as Chair of Street Connect's Board, given how closely we're linked.'

'That makes sense,' I agreed.

'Marvellous!' he said, grinning. 'Alistair's already agreed.'

'Brilliant!' I replied, genuinely pleased.

Peter's face turned reflective. 'Have I ever told you how Alistair's succession came about?'

'I don't think so.'

His eyes twinkled as he leaned in. 'Well, it happened like this . . . "Alistair Matheson will follow you in Glasgow City Church." That's what I heard at 3 a.m. on Tuesday, 3rd July 2012.'

He chuckled. 'Do you know how I responded? Rolled over in bed and muttered, "What was that about? Too much cheese? Get back to sleep, you idiot. And anyway, what kind of man would leave Skye to move to Glasgow?"'

I burst out laughing. 'And what happened next?'

'Well, later that morning, I was leading a gathering of Scottish Apostolic Church leaders in Perth. And guess who was there?'

'Alistair,' I said, already hooked.

Peter's face lit up. 'Yes! I could hardly believe it. I barely knew him – we'd only met briefly once before. But there he was. So, I started the meeting, and after worship, I opened the floor for prayer requests.'

'Let me guess – he asked for prayer?'

Peter nodded. 'He did, and said he and his wife had left Glasgow nineteen years earlier on a word from the Lord. They'd planted a church and served in Skye nearly two decades. But now, their twenty years would be up in 2014, and they were seeking God's guidance for what was next.'

I leaned back, stunned. 'That's incredible.'

'And I had no idea they were originally from Glasgow!' Peter shook his head. 'You can imagine my jaw dropping. First, that word in the night, and then Alistair sharing this, just hours later. I was speechless. And then came the regret – realising I'd dismissed a divine revelation as a disruption to my sleep.'

'What did you do?'

'During the coffee break, I spoke to two trusted brothers. Then at lunch, I pulled Alistair aside and told him about the dream. And do you know what? He was just as amazed as I was.'

I shook my head in awe. 'That's amazing, Peter. No doubt about it – Alistair was meant to be your successor.'

'Absolutely. I used to think a healthy ministry should raise up its own successor from within. But on this occasion, who am I to argue with God?'

***

'Alistair, I've been thinking a lot about my role,' I said, my voice laced with both excitement and hesitation. We had just settled into our usual spot by the window in Costa, overlooking George Square, now bathed in the golden glow of autumn.

'Oh?' he said, eyebrows raised. 'Tell me more.'

I exhaled slowly. 'Well, now we have Julie and two other part-time staff members on board, I've been realising something. Supporting and developing the team is just as important as my role in reaching and supporting the people we serve.'

'Absolutely,' Alistair said, nodding. 'And those leadership and management courses you've done will serve you – and them – really well.'

'Exactly.' I nodded. 'And it's made me realise – I'm at a crossroads.'

Alistair leaned in. 'What do you mean?'

I took a sip of my latte, eyes drifting briefly to the street. 'As leadership responsibilities grow, so does the number of people we're supporting. And if we're serious about reaching more areas of the city, something's got to give.

Either I step fully into leading the charity and let go of some direct outreach and support responsibilities, or we find someone else to lead while I stay on the front line.'

I pointed outside. 'I mean, this is my passion. It's why I started all this.' I shook my head, conflicted. 'But if we're really going to live out the vision – "empowering the local church to reach the lost" – then something has to shift. And I think I know what that is.'

Alistair leaned forward, his expression intense. 'Ricky, bringing someone else in to lead isn't the answer. You're the one carrying this vision. You're God's man for the job.'

His words struck something deep. I looked up and nodded. 'That's exactly what I've been thinking too. Aye, it feels like a sacrifice – stepping back from outreach work – but if it means equipping more churches, helping more people, then it's worth it.'

'Which is why you need to step fully into leadership,' he said firmly. 'You carry the vision, and the Board trusts you to take it forward.'

Alistair, like Peter, was a visionary. It's one of the reasons we got on so well. He carried this infectious faith – bold, pioneering, full of fire. The kind of leadership that made the impossible seem achievable. And it was becoming clearer by the minute – he was the right person to chair the Board through this next season.

'So, with that in mind,' I continued, 'I've been thinking about the need for clearer staff roles. If we want to grow, we can't just keep running with "everyone does a bit of everything". We need to position people where they thrive.'

'That's leadership, Ricky,' Alistair said with quiet affirmation. 'What are you thinking?'

'Well, I need to fully step into a project manager role. We need defined support worker posts – Julie could take on their supervision. And we also need an administrator and a fundraiser.'

'That's a great plan. Let's take it to the next Board meeting.'

He paused, then pulled out his phone. 'What you're saying reminds me of a verse about Christian leadership.' He opened his Bible app and read:

> 'So Christ himself gave the apostles, the prophets, the evangelists, the pastors and teachers, to equip his people for works of service, so that the body of Christ may be built up.'
>
> *(Ephesians 4:11–12)*

I'd read that passage dozens of times before, but now it hit differently. Like God was bringing it to life in a new way.

Alistair looked up. 'Take the evangelist, for example. It's not just about doing evangelism yourself – it's about equipping others to do it. That's how the Church grows.'

Boom. The words landed hard. This wasn't just a shift in responsibility – it was a shift in calling.

'Ricky, you are an evangelist,' he said, locking eyes with me.

I nodded slowly, sensing something significant was coming.

'Would you pray about being ordained as an evangelist in the Apostolic Church?'[14]

I blinked. 'What?' The question caught me completely off guard.

'Yes, Ricky. I've been watching you. It's obvious to everyone. You're already living this out through Street Connect. All I'd be doing is formalising what's already there.'

I sat up straighter, heart pounding.

'I don't know what to say,' I replied. 'I'm honoured you'd even consider that. Of course I'd need to speak with Julie – and pray.'

14. Apostolic Church UK – Official website: *About Us* https://www.apostolic-church.org/about-us (accessed August 2025).

'Of course,' he said.

'But . . . my immediate response? Aye, I'd love to.' The words felt right even as I said them. 'What would it involve?'

'Not a huge change. It would mostly outwork through what you're already doing here.'

I leaned back, a smile creeping in. 'It makes sense. And I do sense God's leading in all this.' I shook my head with a laugh. 'Still – not quite as dramatic as how God led you to Glasgow City Church and Street Connect!'

Alistair laughed. 'Ah – Peter's told you that, has he?'

'He sure did! Quite the story.'

Alistair's eyes drifted to the window, caught in the memory. 'It was May 2012. My wife and I had just got home from church on a sunny Sunday afternoon in Portree. I remember saying, "I think our time here is nearly up."'

I leaned in.

'A month later, just before a leaders' gathering in Perth, I said to her, "We've probably got a year or two left. Among these leaders are some of the fathers in our movement – why don't I share our prayer request? If they hear anything, great. If not, at least they'll pray."'

I nodded, gripped.

'So just before the coffee break, I shared the request. And that's when Peter – sitting right beside me – nearly choked. His eyes welled up and he pulled a couple of leaders aside.'

'Because that very morning, he'd heard from God that you were his successor,' I said.

'Exactly. And do you know what he said to God at the time? "Lord, Alistair will never leave Skye!"' He laughed. 'But God had other plans. I went to Perth with a prayer request, and came home with a calling. We marvelled – how God had sent us from Glasgow, and how now he was calling us home.'

I shook my head in wonder. 'That's amazing, Alistair. And I, for one, am so glad he did.'

***

'Me? An ordained minister?' I laughed, shaking my head as I recounted my conversation with Alistair to Julie.

'I mean, I know you originally wanted to marry a "pastor",' I teased, shooting her a playful grin, 'but would you settle for an evangelist instead?'

Julie smirked, rolling her eyes. 'I suppose I could make do,' she quipped, before we both burst out laughing.

As the laughter faded, I exhaled, my tone shifting. 'No, but seriously – what do you think?'

Her expression softened as she met my gaze. 'Ricky, I completely agree with Alistair,' she said without hesitation. 'You are an evangelist. This calling has been obvious for a long time. I think you should go for it.'

I held her words for a moment, letting their weight settle. And deep down, I knew she was right.

After more prayer and reflection, we sensed God's leading in it – how it aligned with everything else that was unfolding: the ordination, the shift in my role, and the growing responsibilities at Street Connect. It wasn't about a title; it was confirmation of the direction God was already leading us.

Earlier that year, Alistair had invited me onto the church leadership team, and I'd accepted. That step led to my ordination as an elder. Now, with increasing responsibilities – at Street Connect, spiritually, and at home with our growing family – I could see the bigger picture taking shape.

The truth was undeniable: to carry all that God had entrusted to me – my family, my ministry, and this expanding vision – I would need to keep growing. As a leader. As a father. As a man called to serve.

And I was ready.

Chapter 12

When God Steps In

'So, what do you think?' I asked, leaning forward, hands clasped, as we debriefed after interviewing candidates for our first-ever fundraising role.

Peter exhaled, rubbing his chin. 'Well, those last two were head and shoulders above the rest. But they're both so good. How do we choose?'

'I know,' I said, shaking my head. 'It's a tough one. They both bring so much to the table.'

'It's a shame we can't take them both on,' Peter added, glancing around the room.

I let out a small chuckle, though I felt the same tension. 'I know. But the reality is we've only got enough in the budget to hire one of them part-time for six months – and even that's tight. We'd need to see a pretty quick return on investment—'

Before I could finish, Alistair leaned in, his voice steady and clear. 'I don't think it's a question of whether we can afford to hire them both. It's whether we can afford *not* to.'

The room fell silent. His words landed like a lead weight – bold, confronting, and deeply challenging.

I looked at him, then nodded slowly. 'You're right. It would stretch us financially, no doubt. But what if this is the investment that unlocks the growth we need?'

Peter's face lit up. 'So . . . we go for it?'

I took a deep breath. The logic said no. But something in my spirit stirred. 'Aye. Let's do it. I'll call them both and offer them the job.'

And just like that, we took a double step of faith. We didn't have all the money, but we had a strong sense that God was in it.

It was a bold decision. One that would stretch us. But one that would soon prove to be a turning point in the life of Street Connect.

We closed out our third financial year with an income of £87,105.

And things were about to change – dramatically.

But not before we faced one of the toughest decisions yet . . .

'Hello, Ricky speaking. How can I help?'

'Hi, Ricky, I'm calling from The Johnstone Foundation.'

I sat up straighter. This didn't feel like a routine check-in. 'Ah, good to hear from you. What can I do for you?'

'I'll get straight to the point. As you know, your three-year funding agreement is due to finish in a few months.'

'That's right.'

'Well, we're really pleased with the work Street Connect is doing and the impact you're making in Glasgow city centre. In fact, we're open to offering a two-year extension.'

A grin spread across my face. 'That's amazing news – thank you!'

But then, a shift in tone.

'There's just one thing you need to be aware of . . .'

My smile faded. 'Okay . . .'

'We've recently changed our giving strategy.'

A quiet unease crept in. 'Go on.'

'We've noticed your staff roles carry a General Occupational Requirement for a live and active Christian faith.'

'That's right – fully compliant with the Equalities Act.'

'Yes, we understand. But we've made a policy change. We no longer fund positions that carry either a religious or political requirement.'

His words landed like a blow to the chest.

I turned towards the window, my eyes settling on the City Chambers at the bottom of the hill. A swirl of thoughts rushed in. This wasn't just about funding. This was about our identity.

He continued. 'If you remove the requirement from your job descriptions, we can continue funding. If not . . . I'm afraid we won't be able to support you going forward.'

I gripped the phone tighter. Part of me wanted to buy time. Just say yes and sort it later. After all, the role in question was mine – they funded half my salary. And they were our biggest funder.

Technically, I wasn't going anywhere. But this wasn't about technicalities. It was about who we were.

I'd seen it before – once-faith-filled organisations slowly watering down their convictions. One small compromise at a time.

Was this that moment for us?

I exhaled. No. We'd be cutting out the heart of who we are.

'I'll need to speak with our Board,' I said, steadying my voice. 'But my gut says we can't make that change. I'll come back to you once we've had time to consider.'

'Of course. Let me know.'

The call ended. I sat back, staring out the window. My heart was heavy. There was no backup funder waiting in the wings. We'd just taken on new staff. The timing couldn't have been worse.

We prayed. We discussed. And the Board came to a unanimous decision: we would not remove the requirement.

I called back and gave our response. As expected, the funding would end. They could no longer support any posts that carried a faith requirement – including mine.

I hung up, feeling the uncertainty cling like a fog.

But then March came. And with it – provision like we'd never seen before.

In that one month alone, we received £77,500 – nearly the equivalent of our entire income for the previous year.

Stunned, I looked out that same window again, as a whisper rose in my heart: *You are not reliant on any funder. I have deeper pockets than they do.*

Peace washed over me.

This hadn't just been a test. It had been a lesson in trust. And just when I thought the story was done, the phone rang again.

'Hello, Ricky speaking.'

'Hi, Ricky, it's me again – from The Johnstone Foundation.'

I braced myself.

'I spoke with our Board. We've made an exception. We'd like to continue supporting your work for another two years – as long as the funds aren't used for staff salaries.'

I let out a breath I didn't realise I'd been holding. 'That's brilliant news. Thank you so much. Please pass on our thanks to your Board.'

In the end, we still received funding – albeit less – but it validated our decision. And it confirmed something far more important:

We are not dependent on organisations.

We are dependent on God.

Between the decision to stand firm, the incredible giving in March, and the bold hires we'd made the previous year, something was shifting.

That financial year, our income rose to £277,635 – more than triple the previous year.

The fundraising team had worked hard.

But we all knew the truth.

This was God.

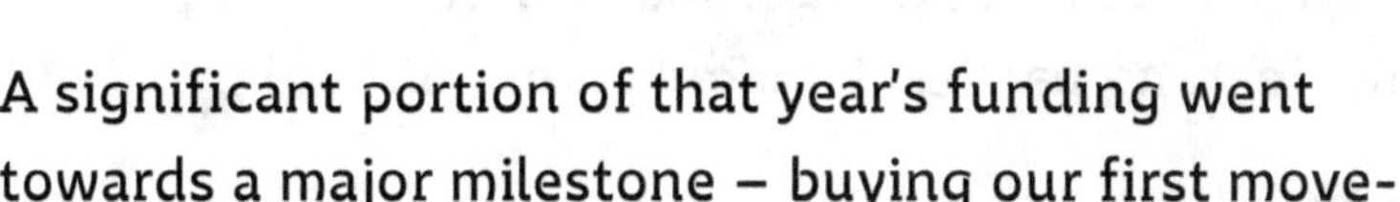

A significant portion of that year's funding went towards a major milestone – buying our first move-on flat. It marked a crucial step in strengthening our aftercare support.

In the summer of 2017, we secured a two-bedroom property and were finally ready to welcome our first residents.

The first to move in was Roger, who we had earlier helped get into rehab. Seeing him take this next step was an incredibly proud moment. He now had a stable base to rebuild his life.

And what made it even more special was what happened next.

When I later left my paid role with Bethany, Roger stepped into my job. Then, when he moved on, his first flatmate, Jamie, took on the role after him. A full-circle moment. A living example of transformation.

But before either of them reached that point, their journey of recovery continued in our move-on flats – safe, supported, and structured spaces where they could take real steps towards independence and lasting stability.

I remember one afternoon sitting with Jamie in my office.

'So, tell me a bit about your journey out of addiction,' I said, leaning back as I looked across at Jamie.

He exhaled slowly, a smile flickering briefly before fading. 'Aye, no worries. I grew up in a good home. Great holidays, lots of laughs . . .' He paused, his gaze lowering. 'Plenty of wee gems and diamonds that got buried beneath years of addiction.'

I nodded, feeling the weight in his voice.

'Life started off good, but the choices I made pulled me into this cycle I couldn't escape. Before I knew it, I was convinced there was no way out.'

His voice grew quieter. 'Addiction stripped everything, man. Self-worth. Confidence. I was carrying all these internal wounds nobody could see.'

He glanced up. 'Folk talk about trauma being the reason people use drugs – and aye, that's true for some. But for me? The lifestyle itself was the trauma. That world – it isolates you. It consumes you.'

I nodded again. 'I get that.'

Jamie gave a small laugh. 'I remember a doctor saying to me, right in the middle of the chaos, "If you could channel all that energy into something good instead of drugs, your life would be completely different."'

I smiled. 'Sounds like he was onto something.'

'Aye,' he laughed. 'Sometimes I wonder if he was a Christian and God was speaking through him.'

Then his tone shifted – lighter now. 'Everything changed when I came to faith in Jesus. That's what led me to rehab.'

I nodded. 'I remember when you started volunteering with us, before going to the Teen Challenge Leadership Academy.'

'Aye,' he said, his eyes bright. 'I knew God had called me to work with broken people. That's why I did the internship with you guys – to learn more.'

Jamie went on to complete the internship, move on from the flat, and later join our team part-time as a project worker, balancing that with three days a week at Bethany.

Looking back, he once told me, 'That flat was a stepping stone, man. It helped me move forward – spiritually and practically. I was surrounded by people who backed me. I'm better off for it.'

He smiled. 'Now I'm working full-time with Bethany as a recovery and resettlement worker. And I thank God every day that I get to use all the broken stuff from my past to give hope to others.'

His grin widened. 'Since moving out, I've bought my own wee place. I got married last year, and we're about to have our first kid together!'

Then, with a look of joy, he added, 'And I hit a big milestone – ten years clean last October. I fully believe there's life after addiction.'

A mischievous twinkle sparked in his eye. 'And as you know, I grew to love the mountains. My life's gone from valley to mountaintop. So to celebrate, I climbed all two hundred and eighty-two Scottish Munros – in just three years!'

I laughed, shaking my head. 'What an achievement, Jamie.'

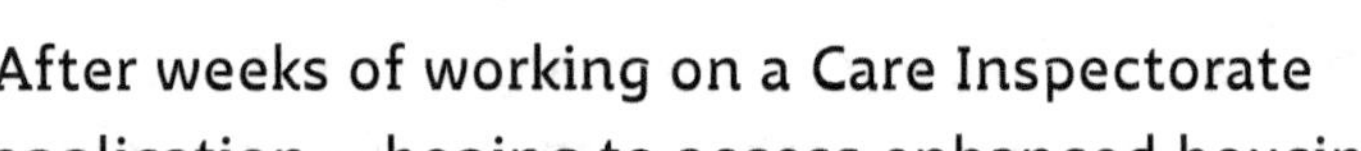

After weeks of working on a Care Inspectorate application – hoping to access enhanced housing benefit and increase income beyond just rent – my phone buzzed.

'Hello, is this Ricky McAddock?'

'Yes, speaking,' I replied, adjusting in my chair.

'I'm calling from Glasgow City Council. You recently submitted a Housing Benefit claim, and your application's been passed to our team – we handle all charity-related claims.'

'Ah, okay,' I said, slightly puzzled. 'We're just about to finish an application to the Care Inspectorate so we can apply for enhanced Housing Benefit.'

'Oh, you don't need to do that.'

I paused. 'We don't?'

'No. A lot of charities are now coming straight through us. You can apply directly instead.'

Now I was really confused. 'Really? That's not what we've been told. All the guidance we've received points to going through the Care Inspectorate.'

'Nope. You can apply straight to us. More and more charities are doing it this way.'

I leaned back in my chair, slowly running a hand over my face. This would save us hours of time, reduce our compliance responsibilities, and free up capacity we badly needed.

'Right . . . okay. Can I get back to you later in the week?'

'Of course, no problem at all.'

'Thanks for the call. I'll be in touch soon.'

I hung up and sat there for a moment, staring at the wall.

Was this God's provision again?

We'd spent months planning around the Care Inspectorate process – gathering policies, structuring our support to meet requirements. And now, out of nowhere, a simpler route was opening up.

I started making calls – double checking with key contacts in the sector. No red flags. All the signs pointed to green.

A week later, we submitted our rent sheet. It was approved quickly.

A council officer came to inspect the flat, ask questions, and verify our support model. Everything passed.

Since then, we've built a strong relationship with the council, and they've extended the same financial support to all of our move-on flats.

At the time of writing, we now have four flats with seven bed spaces. Since opening our first flat, 70 per cent of residents have moved on to positive destinations, such as employment, further education, and independent living.

We're now actively seeking investment to expand further. This has become a vital part of our work, one that we've been able to grow with surprising ease – thanks to that unexpected phone call.

***

Let me wrap up this section on our move-on flats with one of those undeniable 'this has to be God' moments – this time, in the form of an unexpected recruitment story.

By this point, it was glaringly obvious – we needed someone with real housing expertise. None of our staff or Trustees had a housing background, and as the work expanded, we needed to fill this gap.

So, we decided to advertise for a part-time housing support coordinator.

We had a specific wish list:

1. Someone with housing experience.
2. Someone with the skills to support people in recovery.
3. And, if that wasn't specific enough, someone with a strong Christian faith, in line with our occupational requirement.

I still remember the scepticism from a few trusted voices: 'Perhaps you're asking for too much. You'll never find someone with all three.'

We wrestled with whether to broaden the criteria, but, in the end, we decided to stick to our convictions and trust God would bring the right person.

So, we put out the job ad and waited . . .

And waited.

It's fair to say the floodgates did not open. In fact, we received just one application.

But here's the thing – that one applicant?

- Was a qualified housing officer.
- Had recently completed a counselling qualification.
- And, of course, was a committed Christian.

It was as if the job description had been written just for her.

I remember reading her application and shaking my head with a smile. 'Of course. This has to be God.'

Looking back, it was yet another moment that confirmed what we were learning over and over: when God is leading, he brings the right people, at the right time, in the right way.

***

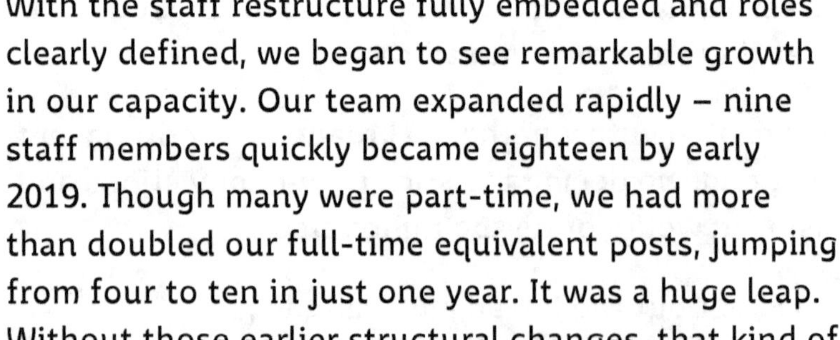

With the staff restructure fully embedded and roles clearly defined, we began to see remarkable growth in our capacity. Our team expanded rapidly – nine staff members quickly became eighteen by early 2019. Though many were part-time, we had more than doubled our full-time equivalent posts, jumping from four to ten in just one year. It was a huge leap. Without those earlier structural changes, that kind of growth simply wouldn't have been possible.

As the team grew, so did my role. I often joke that hiring people who were way more competent than me in their specialist areas only highlighted how bad I had been at a lot of the things I had to juggle in the early days – even the direct support of participants! Thankfully, with a larger team came a stronger, more structured approach to managing volunteers, which had also surged to around fifty regular volunteers.

Hiring more staff was never the goal in itself. But each new role meant more people reached, more lives transformed. Watching Street Connect become a platform for others to step into their calling – giving their best time to addiction recovery ministry – was one of the greatest joys of this season, and continues to be.

And as our internal capacity grew, our outward vision was already beginning to take shape.

We had begun to look outward – to churches and communities crying out for hope. The vision of partnering with local churches to reach the lost was no longer just a dream. It was becoming central to who we were.

The next chapter of our journey was clear: it was time to multiply.

Chapter 13

The Local Church: The Hope of the World

'I love it, Ricky! What about your first partnership being in Possilpark?' Mark exclaimed, his excitement unmistakable.

'The church you planted?' I asked, curiosity fully piqued.

'Yes! You should speak to one of the leaders who took over after I moved on. You've been to the church, you've seen the area – you know how bad the drug problem is.'

'I do, Mark,' I said, shaking my head. 'Honestly, I don't think there's anywhere in Glasgow that needs this more. I still remember heading up there in my addiction days with a mate to buy a big package of heroin. The whole thing ran like a well-oiled machine – it was so organised.'

Mark sighed. 'Yeah, it's heart-breaking. But that's exactly why Street Connect could make a difference in Possil.'

'I couldn't agree more,' I said, my mind already racing. 'Can you connect me with someone?'

'Absolutely,' he replied without hesitation.

And just like that, Possilpark became our first church partnership. By January 2017, we had officially launched, offering street outreach and a drop-in café every Friday afternoon.

The impact was immediate. People engaged, lives were touched, and some even began attending our community recovery programme in the city centre.

One of those people was Charlie.

'Charlie, I have to say – I'm really impressed with how engaged you've been. You've hardly missed a session! That's rare for the group.'

We both chuckled.

'Ricky, I just want to get to rehab. I'm determined,' he replied, his voice full of urgency and hope.

'I can see that,' I nodded. We were in my office for one of our regular one-to-one sessions. 'So, that's not a Glasgow accent I'm hearing – how did you end up in Possil?'

He glanced down, voice softening. 'I moved from Aberdeen when I was thirty-one to go to rehab. My best pal had just died of an overdose.'

I felt my stomach drop. 'That's devastating, Charlie. I'm so sorry.'

'Aye. I'd already lost so many friends to drugs. If I didn't change, I'd be next. Back then, I was on methadone, Valium and heroin. My life was an endless cycle – addiction, homelessness, overdoses, prison, repeat.'

I nodded slowly. 'That's a brutal cycle to be caught in. Were any family still in your life through all that?'

He looked up. 'I've got a daughter, an older sister, and a younger brother.' He paused.

I waited, sensing more behind the silence. 'Your parents?' I asked gently.

His eyes dropped again. ' I don't remember much from my early years. My dad drank a lot. My mum and dad fought constantly – mostly about money, or the lack of it. One day, when I was about six, my mum walked out. Left a note on the fireplace. My sister – just a year older – was left to look after us.'

I felt a lump rise in my throat. 'That's a lot for a wee boy to carry.'

'Aye. My dad tried, but with the drink and unpaid rent, the council eventually stepped in and took us into care.'

He sighed. 'We were placed with a foster family at first. It was okay for a while, but they had more kids, and we started acting out. They couldn't cope. After that, it was children's homes, then more foster placements. I started stealing, drinking, using. By fifteen, I was kicked out. By eighteen, I'd already served my first prison sentence. That's where I started injecting heroin.'

I sat back, letting the weight of his story settle. 'You've come through more than most ever see.'

'It was grim,' he said. 'My daughter was born when I was twenty-two. I wanted to get clean for her, but I couldn't break free. It was the same cycle – drugs, crime, prison.'

I nodded. 'I know how that feels.'

'That's why I went to rehab originally. But I hadn't dealt with the root issues. I fell back into it – first drink, then methadone and Valium again. For years, I was stuck.'

He looked me in the eye. 'Then my partner got sick – motor neurone disease. I tried to care for her, but she passed away. After that, I tried to come off methadone on my own. The doctors warned me, but I didn't care. I ended up sectioned in a psychiatric unit.'

He took a shaky breath. 'When I got out, I walked through the doors of the church in Possilpark. That was January 2014. By April, I'd given my life to Christ. By November, I was baptised. I was forty-five.'

'That's incredible,' I said, deeply moved. 'But I know the journey doesn't end there. Faith doesn't always mean instant freedom from addiction.'

'Exactly. I couldn't break free at first. I didn't even notice the changes happening. But something had shifted.'

I leaned in. 'Let's build on that. Let's get you back to rehab – this time, make it the last.'

We both laughed, but we knew it wouldn't be easy.

Charlie was still on a high dose of methadone and using street Valium. He was so desperate, he tried detoxing on his own – again landing him in psychiatric care with drug-induced psychosis.

I remember calling one of the church leaders. 'I don't know if Charlie's going to make it. It's touch and go.'

'I know,' he said. 'But he's so determined.'

'He really is,' I said. 'If we pull the rug now, he could lose hope. Let's keep pushing forward and see what happens.'

Miraculously, that was the turning point.

His drugs worker helped him taper from 150ml to 30ml of methadone. He stopped using street Valium. And after months of determination, he was accepted into rehab with Teen Challenge in Nottingham.

It taught me something I'll never forget: never give up on someone, no matter how hopeless it looks.

Several years later, Charlie reflected:

> 'Through the church, Street Connect, Teen Challenge, and the life-changing power of the gospel, I was loved back to life. God restored my mind, my health, and my family. My daughter, who I hadn't seen in ten years, is back in my life.
>
> 'I've now been clean for nearly nine years. I work for a homeless charity, helping others rebuild their lives. I'm also part of a church plant in Tranent, East Lothian, where we've moved into a housing scheme to reach the local community.
>
> 'God's blessed me with a wife, three step-kids, and two grandkids.
>
> 'I used to think my life was over. Now I know – with God, there's always a way forward.'

Charlie's story is one I'll never forget. From addiction to transformation. From prison to purpose. From hopelessness to hope.

As we refined the lessons from our first partnership in Possilpark, we felt a strong pull towards an area that held deep personal meaning for Julie and me – Govan, our own community.

We had already built a strong relationship with a local pastor there, a Govan lad himself, who had planted a church the same year we launched Street Connect. Like us, he had a heart for those in addiction.

'This just makes so much sense,' he said over coffee one morning, his thick Govan accent full of conviction. 'We're already reaching out to folk struggling with addiction, but we can't do this alone.'

It was clear this would be a natural fit, mirroring what we'd done in Possilpark. Within a few months, we had launched a drop-in café and street outreach in the area. The impact was immediate. Within six months, thirty to forty people were regularly attending the café each week.

The pastor later reflected, 'This is probably the best project we've launched since the church began. We're making loads of new connections in the community, and some folk are even integrating into the church. It's been a game changer.'

But the momentum didn't stop there.

The following year, three more churches came on board – two in Greater Glasgow, and one in Deal, Kent.

If you're not familiar with UK geography, Deal is a seaside town on the south coast of England – nearly the opposite end of the country from Glasgow!

It wasn't long before our staff started joking, 'Send me to Deal, Ricky – I feel called to the sunny south coast!'

And whenever I shared our partner locations, the same question came up time and again: 'How on earth did you end up in Deal?'

Here's how.

Alistair, our chair at the time, also served on the national leadership team of the Apostolic Church UK. Through that role, an unexpected opportunity opened up – one that would take Street Connect far beyond what we had envisioned.

At a national church event, Alistair got chatting to a pastor from Deal. As he shared about Street Connect's work, something sparked. The senior pastor explained they already had someone on their staff team who came from an addiction background and came to faith in Jesus, resulting in a complete life transformation. He was now their community pastor and had been running a drop-in café. They were now looking to take the work further.

'Do you think we could become part of Street Connect?' he asked.

Soon after, I found myself in conversation with Alistair and the leadership from Deal. The more we talked, the more it became clear – this could work.

The fit felt right.

I paused. 'Expanding this far south wasn't part of our immediate plan. We saw this kind of growth as something for further down the line. But . . . if you're willing, so are we. Just know, it might be a bit bumpy – we've never done this before.'

They smiled. 'We're ready.'

And that was it. We prayed together, committed in principle, and began the formal process of establishing our first church partnership outside Scotland. After completing training and preparation, we officially launched Street Connect in Deal in June 2018 – building on the strong foundation already in place.

The momentum didn't slow. In 2019, two more partnerships emerged, both in the Greater Glasgow and Clyde area.

By this point, a pattern had become clear: three of the five new partnerships during this period could be traced back to one key person – Alistair.

Through his national leadership role, Alistair had become the architect behind some of our most significant expansions – including Greenock.

And that's where Alex comes in.

***

'Ricky, I genuinely believe the local church is the hope for our nation – and the greatest untapped community asset our country has.' Alex's voice carried conviction as he leaned forward in his chair. 'If we can marry the compassion and goodwill of the Church with Street Connect's expertise in addiction recovery, we could see some of the most broken communities truly transformed.'

I grinned, feeling his passion. 'That's a great line, Alex. I might have to borrow that one.'

We both laughed.

Sitting across from him in my office, I took a sip of coffee and nodded. 'It's so good having you on the team – your experience is already helping us grow and develop.'

Alex's expression turned thoughtful. 'It's an honour, Ricky. For years, I had to keep my faith and my work in addiction work completely separate. But here, I finally get to combine the two.'

He leaned back, exhaling slowly. 'In my previous role, we followed the "Social Learning" model of addiction. It sees addiction as a learned behaviour that can be unlearned through a bio-psycho-social approach. But there was no space for the spiritual side. That always frustrated me. Leaving out faith felt like trying to fight with one hand tied behind your back.'

I frowned. 'That must've been hard to navigate.'

A knowing smile spread across his face. 'It was. The interesting thing is, when clients found out I was a pastor, they weren't asking me about relapse prevention; they wanted to know about my faith. They were more interested in the hope I carried than the tools I had.'

He chuckled, then quoted from memory: 'Always be prepared to give an answer to everyone who asks you to give the reason for the hope that you have. But do this with gentleness and respect.'[15]

I smiled. 'That's powerful, Alex.'

He nodded. 'Some colleagues were suspicious of my faith, so I had to tread carefully. But now?' His face lit up. 'Now, with Street Connect, I can finally work holistically – bio, psycho, social *and* spiritual. It's what I've always believed in. And now I get to live it out.'

'No more walking on eggshells,' I quipped.

He laughed. 'Exactly.'

I leaned forward. 'So, how did you get into addiction work in the first place?'

Alex's tone shifted. His eyes dropped slightly as he exhaled. 'It started with my own family.'

15. 1 Peter 3:15.

I sat up straighter. 'Go on.'

'In the '90s, drugs flooded our area. It started with cannabis, but when that dried up, heroin swept in. It hit hard. My eldest son, also called Alex, got caught in it.'

I felt my stomach tighten. 'That must've been heart-breaking.'

'It was,' Alex nodded slowly. 'He fought to get clean. And for a while, he did. But then one night, he was in the wrong place at the wrong time. His tolerance had dropped and he overdosed. He was just nineteen.'

A lump formed in my throat. 'I'm so sorry, Alex.'

He gave a sad smile. 'Thanks. It was the darkest time of our lives. But through the grief, our church pulled together. We knew we had to do something – not just for Alex, but for the whole community. Even before he passed, we had opened a small, faith-based rehab on the Isle of Cumbrae. None of us were specialists – just a bunch of ordinary Christians desperate for change.'

I shook my head in admiration. 'That's incredible.'

'Over time, we rebuilt our lives. I worked in engineering and manufacturing for years. But when the industry collapsed, I found myself unemployed. That was a turning point – God nudging me towards something new. I took a role as a support worker in a local addiction service and, before long, was leading the organisation. Around that time, I was also called into pastoral ministry.'

His eyes met mine. 'It's taken a long time, but for the first time, I'm in a place where faith and addiction recovery can finally work hand in hand. That's what makes this so fulfilling.'

Then he grinned. 'You know what I love most about Street Connect?'

I raised an eyebrow. 'What?'

'You take recycling seriously.'

I blinked. 'Sorry . . . what?'

He chuckled. 'Not just plastic and paper – *people*. The most valuable thing in the world. So many folk that society's written off get a second chance here. They get clean, volunteer, gain confidence – and before you know it, they're on staff. What is it – about half the team that now has personal lived experience of addiction?'

I grinned. 'You've done your homework. That's right. It's what gives our work such depth and impact – people who've lived through the chaos, reaching out to help others.'

A year or two after that conversation, I visited Alex's church in Greenock, where we'd launched another thriving partnership. I preached at their Sunday service and stayed for the community meal afterwards.

As I sat in the main church hall, I looked around and felt something stir deep within me.

I leaned over to Alex and whispered, 'Look at this. People from all walks of life – eating, talking, sharing. This is how church should be.'

He smiled knowingly. 'That's what it's all about, Ricky.'

I nodded, taking in the scene. 'This is why we do what we do.'

As I looked around the room, I felt a deep sense of gratitude welling up inside me. The air buzzed with conversation and laughter, the clinking of cutlery against plates filling the space with warmth. What struck me most was the diversity – people in addiction, now sitting side by side with lifelong church members, professionals, families, and people from all walks of life.

This was true community.

I sat back, breathed in the moment, and smiled.

This was church.

And as the church partnership work continued to gather momentum, I sensed Street Connect was on the brink of something even greater. We were no longer just expanding locally – we were beginning to think nationally.

And that kind of growth would demand more.

More from the organisation.

More from me.

I could feel it stirring – something shifting inside, readying me for what was to come.

It was time to rise to the challenge.

Chapter 14

The Making of a Leader

There are moments in life when you look back and realise that what once felt like ruin was actually the raw material of purpose. I resonate deeply with a story about Michelangelo – not just because of its brilliance, but because it speaks to my own becoming. What others overlooked, God repurposed. What others saw as too flawed, he called his own.

Michelangelo's early life was marked by hardship. Born into a family that had fallen from minor nobility, his father's financial mismanagement left them impoverished. As a result, young Michelangelo was handed over to a wet nurse from a family of stone masons. Later in life, he reflected that even as an infant, he had been surrounded by the very material that would define his destiny. In his words, he was breathing marble dust and drinking it with his nurse's milk.

Years on, a massive block of marble lay abandoned in Florence. Known as *il gigante* – the giant – it had been rejected by master sculptors as too flawed to work with.[16] Two of the best in the Renaissance had attempted it and failed. It was considered too brittle, unpredictable, liable to crack under pressure. A block with promise, perhaps, but one that simply couldn't be shaped.

Then came Michelangelo. At just twenty-six, he accepted the challenge others had walked away from – beating even Leonardo da Vinci to the commission. Where others saw problems, he saw potential. With painstaking skill and divine inspiration, he brought forth a masterpiece: the statue of *David*. The shepherd boy, poised and ready – not only faced a giant, he had been carved *from* one. Even the oversized hand, Michelangelo said, was a symbol: God's power at work through the unlikely.

I take comfort from this story when I realise that the unwanted stone had been left wasting its potential for decades. Like me – nearly thirty years. But perhaps the same hand of providence, holding the reins of both destiny and fate, might once again use the darkness of my addiction to produce not only meaning out of misery, but beauty out of ashes – daring not just to explain the darkness of my life, but to create a work that redeems it.

***

16. Michelangelo's *David*, Accademia Gallery – Official website: *The History of the David* https://www.accademia.org/explore-museum/artworks/michelangelos-david/ (accessed August 2025).

'Ricky, it sounds like you're in a leadership transition season,' Mark said, looking up from the paperwork we'd been poring over.

I frowned, intrigued. 'What do you mean, Mark?'

'If you look here,' he said, tapping his finger on a highlighted passage, 'Dr Clinton describes a leadership transition where your focus shifts from leadership development to a dual focus – *spiritual formation* and *strategic leadership*.'[17]

I nodded slowly. 'The strategic leadership part, aye, that resonates. But spiritual formation?' I hesitated. 'I mean, I worked on that a lot at Teen Challenge. That's where I built my foundation.'

Mark looked at me for a moment before leaning forward. 'I don't think you're fully grasping what spiritual formation means, are you?'

'Well . . .' I stalled.

'Have you heard the term before?'

'I mean, isn't it just about our initial formation in Christ?'

'That's part of it,' Mark acknowledged, 'but it's also so much more. It's a lifelong journey of deepening your relationship with God, becoming more like Jesus in character, and–'

17. Robert J. Clinton, *The Making of a Leader: Recognizing the Lessons and Stages of Leadership Development* (Colorado Springs: NavPress, 2012).

I cut in, 'I get that, and I'm committed to it, but it's the strategic leadership part that really excites me.'

Mark smiled knowingly. 'I can see why, Ricky. You've done such a great job growing Street Connect into what it is today, and you've grown so much as a leader over these past four years we've been working together.'

'And you've played a big role in that,' I said gratefully. 'Those personality profiling tools you introduced me to really helped me understand who I am and how God has wired me. Seeing how I'm naturally wired for leadership. And the advice, the connections – you've been instrumental in shaping me.'

'And the way you consume all those leadership books,' he chuckled. 'I mean, haven't you read almost all of John Maxwell's books?'

'Pretty much,' I laughed.

Still smiling, Mark grew serious again. 'Ricky, I've rarely met anyone as committed to personal growth as you. Your drive to reach more communities – it's remarkable.'

I nodded. 'Well, as you know, two of my biggest strengths are "learner" and "achiever". That inner drive pushes me forward – I can't help it.'

We both laughed, but Mark gently brought the conversation back. 'And that's exactly why you need to embrace this transition season. If you're going to fulfil the vision God's given you, your development focus has to shift.'

I let his words settle. He was right.

Breaking the silence, Mark added, 'I think we're both sensing that our mentoring relationship is coming to an end.'

I nodded. 'Aye, I think so too.'

'With me moving away from Glasgow, I feel like I've played my part in your leadership journey. But I'd love to help you take the next steps by introducing you to two people: one who can walk with you in the area of spiritual formation, and the other who can support your strategic leadership growth.'

Now he had my full attention. 'Oh?'

'I'll reach out to Tom. I think he'd be a great fit for where you're at spiritually. He'll help you go deeper, not just in practice but in your inner life with God.'

I felt something stir within me. 'That would be amazing.'

'The work we've done looking at your past – identifying where God has been shaping you – it's powerful,' he said. 'It's what we call "mining your own experience".'

I took a deep breath, feeling a surge of anticipation. 'Thanks, Mark. I'm honestly excited for what's ahead.

And I really appreciate everything you've done to help me reflect on my journey. The good, the bad – it's all shaped me into who I am today.'

Mark nodded, a knowing smile on his face. 'Yep,' he said, leaning back in his chair. 'And God's not done with you yet.'

He paused, then added, 'Tom will be brilliant for you. He'll challenge you, stretch you, and help shape the inner life that will sustain your outer calling. And the other contact I've got in mind for leadership will sharpen your edge in that area too. Between them, you'll be well supported for what lies ahead.'

Feeling both the weight and the wonder of what was to come, I nodded. 'I'm ready,' I said, more to myself than to Mark.

He grinned. 'I know you are.'

* * *

As the train rattled along the tracks towards Glasgow, I gazed out of the window, the city lights flickering like distant stars. My mind was a whirlwind of reflection, tracing back over the past five years of my leadership journey. The formal qualifications in Leadership and Management had been valuable, but what truly stood out were the mentors – the people God had placed in my life at just the right moments.

Talk about divine timing!

One thing had become undeniably clear: the growth of a leader and the growth of their organisation are inseparable. As I developed, so did Street Connect. Every lesson learned, every challenge overcome, every shift in my perspective had a direct impact on the organisation and the people we were reaching.

I recalled one of John Maxwell's core leadership principles, 'The Law of the Lid':

> 'Your leadership ability – for better or worse – always determines your effectiveness and the potential impact of your organisation.'[18]

That truth resonated deeply. I could see it unfolding in my own journey. God was weaving everything together – my strengths, my experiences, my calling – aligning them with his greater purpose for Street Connect.

As I sat on the train, lost in thought, a memory surfaced – one that sent a shiver down my spine. I could almost hear the pastor's voice praying over me at the end of that church service all those years ago, his words ringing with authority and conviction:

> 'I see a treasure chest, locked tight. The devil has kept it shut for too long, but God is about to open it. Inside, there are gifts – gifts that were

18. John C. Maxwell, *The 21 Irrefutable Laws of Leadership: Follow Them and People Will Follow You* (Nashville: Thomas Nelson, 2007).

always meant to be yours. And now, he's ready to release them.'

At the time, those words had stirred something deep within me, but I hadn't fully grasped their significance. Now, as I looked back on my journey – the lessons, the struggles, the growth – it all began to make sense. The lid of that chest had been slowly prised open, and one by one, the gifts were being revealed.

This was it. This was the moment I was stepping into the fullness of what had always been inside me. Not buried. Not lost. Just waiting for the right time.

And that time was now.

I exhaled slowly, a quiet confidence settling over me. This wasn't just about my leadership. It was about something far bigger. And I was ready to step into it.

***

Tom agreed to become my new spiritual formation coach. I remember our first meeting well. He looked at me and asked, 'So, Ricky, have you ever considered going on a spiritual retreat?'

'No, but that sounds great,' I replied enthusiastically – until the reality hit me like a ton of bricks. 'Wait . . . how am I supposed to get that one by my wife?'

Tom chuckled, clearly anticipating my reaction. 'Here's what you need to do,' he said with a sly grin.

'When you get home, say to Julie, "Tom told me how beneficial a spiritual retreat would be. Why don't you go on one first?" Then, once she's had her turn, you get to go.'

Genius. Absolute genius.

When I suggested it to Julie, she didn't even hesitate. I barely got the words out before she was packing her bag and heading out the door! I was left managing the house for a few days, counting down the moments until my turn.

Not long after, I found myself at Braehead House, a peaceful Christian retreat centre tucked away in the South Lanarkshire countryside.[19] The stillness of the place was unlike anything I'd experienced before. No distractions, no noise – just space to be with God. Tom had given me some pointers on how to approach a retreat, but nothing could have prepared me for what I encountered.

That first retreat was life-changing. It felt like a fire had been reignited in my soul – a burning heart experience where I sensed God's presence deeply and unmistakably. I knew straight away this wasn't going to be a one-off. It was going to become a core part of my spiritual rhythms. Ever since then, Julie and I have made it a priority to get away on a two-night retreat

19. Braehead House Christian Retreat Centre – Official website: https://www.braeheadhousescotland.co.uk (accessed August 2025).

twice a year. It's been one of the best things we've done for our spiritual lives.

This emphasis on spiritual formation gave me a broader and richer perspective on the Christian life. I came to understand spiritual formation as the ongoing process of being shaped by God into the likeness of Christ – in heart, mind, and character. From the inside out. It's not a course or a one-time experience, but a lifelong journey of transformation, grounded in intimacy with God.

As Street Connect continued to grow, this broader understanding became essential. We were working with churches from all different backgrounds, employing Christians from a wide range of traditions. Up until this point, my experience had been mostly in Pentecostal and Charismatic circles, so being mentored by Tom, an evangelical Methodist, was invaluable. His guidance helped me appreciate the beauty and depth of the wider Church.

Tom also introduced me to the idea of the journey of the soul – a way of recognising the different stages we move through as we grow in faith. It helped me make sense of the shifts I'd experienced, especially when compared with the leadership journey I'd been on with Mark. Different guides for different seasons – but the same faithful God, shaping it all.

His timing is always perfect.

***

During our monthly check-in meeting, I leaned forward and looked Alistair in the eye. 'You know I've been receiving some strategic leadership mentoring recently?'

He nodded thoughtfully. 'Yes, you've mentioned it a few times.'

I took a breath. 'Well, I've been thinking about something for a while now – a shift in my role. It's time I fully step into the senior leadership position.'

Alistair tilted his head. 'Go on.'

'If we're going to fulfil the vision God's given us, I can't keep managing so many staff directly. We need managers over the various teams so I can focus on directing the organisation and building more capacity.'

I could see Alistair was with me, so I pressed on. 'We've hit a ceiling – and we won't grow any further unless we make this transition.'

After a brief pause, Alistair's expression grew thoughtful. 'This is timely, Ricky. It actually aligns with a transition I've also been praying about. As Street Connect grows and clearly needs more structure, I've been sensing that my time as Chair is coming to an end. The next season requires someone with a different skillset from mine.'

I listened carefully as he continued. 'Alistair Barton is already on the Board and brings years of senior administrative and HR experience. I believe he's the right person to step into that role and help guide us through this next stage of development.'

I nodded slowly, grateful for both his honesty and the clarity of God's timing.

We had already moved from a Board made up mostly of members from our founding church to a more diverse group, each bringing strategic skills to help lead us through the next cycle of growth. Alistair Barton officially became our new Chair, and his calm, professional leadership quickly made an impact.

At the next Board meeting, my proposal for a new management structure was approved. Within a few months, we had formed our first-ever Street Connect leadership team.

As I reflected on the change, I saw how vital it was to keep evolving as a leader. The principle of learning, unlearning, and relearning had never felt more real. This restructuring wasn't just about shifting roles – it was about positioning Street Connect for the expansion God had in store.

And it was freeing me to lead more strategically – exactly what we needed to take things to the next level.

Returning to the Michelangelo scene from the beginning of this chapter, I now saw myself differently

– not as the artist, but as the sculpture. That rough, unformed block of stone, once dismissed as too flawed, was destined to become *David* – the masterpiece.

God was still at work, chipping away at the hardened edges of my life, refining me through every challenge, every lesson, every moment of surrender. Each strike of his chisel, though sometimes painful, was shaping me into something I could not yet fully see. The masterpiece wasn't finished. Not even close. But I was beginning to recognise the process. Step by step, piece by piece, the vision of who I was created to be was coming into focus.

And just as I was a work in progress, so too was Street Connect. *As goes the leader, so goes the organisation*[20] – a truth I had come to understand deeply. The growth of our mission wasn't just about strategy or expansion; it was about the ongoing transformation within me. As I leaned further into God, the vision continued to unfold – each step building on the last, revealing more of the path ahead.

I was reminded of the words, 'Your word is a lamp for my feet, a light on my path' (Psalm 119:105).

Not a floodlight. Not a full blueprint. Just enough light to take the next step. Progressive revelation.

20. John C. Maxwell, *Leadership Gold: Lessons I've Learned from a Lifetime of Leading* (Nashville: Thomas Nelson, 2008).

God's will wasn't revealed all at once – it came through trust, obedience, and discernment. My role was not to rush ahead or demand to see the finished masterpiece, but to walk in step with him, one illuminated step at a time.

In the fullness of time, the full beauty of the masterpiece – in my life and in Street Connect – would, in time, be revealed.

Chapter 15

Leading From a Place of Listening

'Ricky, I really feel we're about to enter a season of pruning,' Julie said, her voice calm yet certain as we sat together in the office during one of our regular catch-ups.

I looked up, unsettled by the weight in her tone. 'Why do you think that, Julie?'

She exhaled slowly. 'It started during my morning time with God this week. I was reading John 15, where Jesus talks about the vine.'

I nodded. 'Yeah, I love that passage.'

She opened the Bible on her desk, flipping through the pages with quiet purpose. 'It was these verses.' She read aloud:

> 'I am the true vine, and my Father is the gardener. He cuts off every branch in me that bears no fruit, while every branch that does bear fruit he prunes so that it will be even more fruitful.'
>
> *(John 15:1–2)*

She closed the Bible and looked me in the eye. 'I can't shake the sense that Street Connect is about to go through a season of pruning.'

Her words hit something raw in me. *Pruning.* It sounded spiritual, yes – but also painful. I felt my stomach tighten. I knew enough about pruning to know it wasn't gentle. It meant cutting back. Letting go.

Part of me wanted to push the thought aside. We'd worked so hard to build momentum. Things were growing – slowly, yes, but surely. And now this? Another shaking?

But I'd learnt something over the years: when Julie said she was hearing from God, I had to listen.

Still, my mind raced with quiet dread. What would pruning cost us? Who – or what – might we have to let go of?

I sat back, the weight of her words settling in. Then came another phrase I'd been mulling over for months: *leading from a place of listening.*

I remembered a speaker at a conference talking about how true leadership isn't just about vision – it's about discernment. Listening. First to God, then to the people he's placed around you.

Like Julie.

I took a deep breath, trying to steady the unease rising in my chest. 'The timing of this is . . . interesting,' I said quietly.

Julie nodded.

It was January 2020.

And we had no idea what was about to hit.

***

As we approached March 2020, it felt like the pressure was closing in on us from all sides. Finances were tight. Staffing challenges were mounting. Certain projects weren't unfolding as we had hoped. Julie's word about pruning wasn't just a thought anymore – it was something we were living.

Then COVID-19 hit.

Like everyone else, we were thrown into uncertainty. The world shut down overnight, and we had to rethink everything – how to support our participants, how to prepare our staff for homeworking, how to navigate a crisis no one saw coming.

When the first lockdown took effect, we adapted quickly. Our team pivoted, adjusting services to ensure those in need could still access support. We knew how vital this was – if addiction thrives in isolation, then lockdown was about to be devastating for many.

But the strain was real.

Some of our church partnerships struggled to keep going under the weight of restrictions. A few, heartbreakingly, had to close their doors for good. Our plans for raising income were thrown into disarray, leaving us in a difficult financial position.

We had some tough calls to make.

We managed to place only a couple of staff on furlough, while the rest of the team continued working from home – many on reduced hours as finances grew tighter. We tried to hold on, but, as the weeks went by, our leadership team found itself in difficult conversations, seeking God's guidance, praying desperately for provision.

Eventually, we had no choice but to let go of a couple of staff. It was a tough time. The pruning was no longer just a metaphor; it was happening right in front of us.

And yet, the questions lingered. *What about the team? This is their livelihood. How far will the pruning go?* I slept well most nights, but there were moments when those thoughts circled in the quiet – when the weight of responsibility crept in.

But we reminded ourselves of something crucial: the purpose of pruning isn't to destroy – it's to make way for greater fruit.

And as painful as this season was, we clung to the belief that more fruitful days lay ahead.

Little did we know, things were about to take an unexpected turn . . .

***

One afternoon, as I sat in my downstairs office at home, my phone rang unexpectedly. Glancing at the screen, I saw the caller ID – John Kirkby, the founder and leader of Christians Against Poverty.[21]

That's unusual, I thought. *John never just calls out of the blue.*

'Hi, John,' I answered, my curiosity piqued. 'Great to hear from you. Is everything okay?'

'Yeah, absolutely fine,' he replied casually. 'I've got a question for you.'

Now I was intrigued. 'Alright, fire away.'

21. Christians Against Poverty (CAP) – Official website: *About Us* https://capuk.org/about (accessed August 2025).

'What would you do with £100,000?'

I blinked. What?

'Wait – what do you mean?' I asked, sitting up straighter in my chair.

'Well,' he continued, 'I'm on an advisory panel for a Christian funder who's just launched a £10 million COVID response fund, and they're looking for Christian projects to support – so I thought of you.'

'Wow!' I replied, still trying to process what I was hearing.

'Ricky, you know I love what you guys do. Given the size of your charity, I figured this amount sounded about right. So, what do you think?'

I let out a breathless laugh. 'John, that sounds amazing! Thank you so much for thinking of us.'

'There's a short application,' he explained. 'Have a think about how you'd use the money, and let me know. I want to make sure it aligns with the fund so you have the best chance of success.'

'Absolutely,' I assured him. 'We'll get this sorted ASAP.'

As soon as I ended the call, I sprang into action, setting up an urgent Teams meeting with the leadership team. Within a week, we had our application submitted. Now, all we could do was wait.

Thankfully, we didn't have to wait long.

It was during the heatwave of May 2020. I sat in my home office, staring out at the sun-drenched garden while music blasted from neighbouring houses. Everyone seemed to be making the most of furlough – barbecues, laughter, cold drinks in hand. Meanwhile, I was stuck inside, glued to my desk, working through all the changes needed to strengthen our church partnership model.

Then – *ping.*

An email notification.

I glanced at the sender. The funder.

A wave of nervous excitement rolled over me. I hesitated for a second, then clicked it open.

And there it was.

£100,000.

I was stunned.

I shot out of my chair.

'YES!' I shouted, pumping my fist. 'Thank you, Lord!'

I bolted upstairs, barely stopping for breath. 'Julie, you're never going to believe this!'

Moments later, I was on the phone, calling the rest of the leadership team, buzzing with excitement. But I had one more call to make.

'Peter, you'll never guess what's just happened!'

'Oh?' he replied, his tone curious.

'We just landed the £100,000 grant!'

A beat of silence – then, 'That's wonderful, Ricky. Praise God!'

'It really is,' I agreed, still beaming. 'And I have to thank you for connecting me with John in the first place.'

Peter had known John from his years as a pastor in Bradford, where Peter had also helped to launch Transforming Lives for Good (TLG). The previous year, he had introduced me to both John and Tim, the founder of TLG, and I'd travelled down to Bradford to learn from their experience of scaling nationally.

Now, that connection had led to the biggest one-off grant we had ever received.

And that was just the beginning.

Grant after grant started rolling in. The momentum built rapidly, and by the end of the financial year, our annual income had jumped from £345,000 to £582,000 – a staggering 59 per cent increase.

This surge in funding allowed us to grow our frontline team, enabling us to reopen more services and expand our reach. But we didn't stop there. To sustain this level of growth, we made a strategic decision to strengthen our fundraising capacity, increasing our staff team to twenty-two – our largest team to date.

This also meant our infrastructure was being stretched like never before, and we still had a long way to go in terms of the rebuild we had been undertaking.

***

At the start of 2019, we embarked on what would become a three-year development project – one that would lay the foundation for replicating our work with churches across the country. The Deal pilot project on the south coast of England had been a huge success, but it also revealed just how much we needed to do before expanding beyond Greater Glasgow. It ended during COVID, giving us time to focus regionally while preparing for national growth.

We had to learn fast. We benchmarked against organisations that had successfully replicated their models, attended accelerator programmes, and completely overhauled our approach to regional expansion. It was an immense undertaking – demanding relentless effort and an unshakable vision.

But two years in, I was exhausted.

On the outside, I was still functioning – still leading meetings, making decisions, and pushing forward. But inside, something was fraying. The combination of the pandemic, the pace of Street Connect's growth, the weight of church leadership, and family demands left me running on fumes. I'd wake up some mornings already tired, wondering how long I could keep going. A quiet thought began to haunt me: *If I keep going at this pace, I will eventually burn out.*

I wanted to finish well.

The Bible is filled with stories of leaders who didn't. The same was true of many Christian leaders today – burned out, disillusioned, even disqualified. I refused to become another cautionary tale. But to avoid that, I had to act before reaching breaking point.

Then came the catalyst for change – through Julie.

'I don't think I can do this much longer, Ricky,' she admitted one evening as we sat in our living room, the kids finally in bed.

I looked up from my book, surprised by the intensity in her voice. 'Do what?'

'Be at the city centre church,' she said, shaking her head. 'I love the people, but my heart – it's in Govan. This is where we live. This is where we were called. I feel like we should be in church here.'

I sat back, taking in her words. She wasn't wrong.

For eight years, we had poured ourselves into Glasgow City Church and the work of Street Connect. It had been a huge part of our journey. But if I was honest, something had been stirring beneath the surface. Julie's words had unearthed what I had been feeling but hadn't yet admitted:

We needed a shift.

That conversation set everything in motion.

Through prayer and deep reflection, I realised this wasn't just about where we went to church – it was about what I needed to release.

For years, I'd juggled multiple leadership roles: Street Connect, church, family. But the call on my life was becoming clearer, more focused.

If I wanted to lead Street Connect well, and be present with my family, something had to give.

So, after much prayer, I made the decision.

I would step back from church leadership.

It wasn't easy. That role had been an honour, and I had invested deeply in it. But I knew this was the right move – not just for me, but for my family, and for the future of Street Connect.

Yet even then, it wasn't over. A deeper stirring was taking place, one that would not only shape my own journey, but also profoundly impact the future of Street Connect.

***

'Tom, I'm thinking of taking a sabbatical next summer,' I said, leaning forward during one of our regular Zoom calls.

His face lit up. 'Ricky, that would be so good for you – for your walk with God and for Street Connect.'

I exhaled. 'Yeah. The pace I've been moving at and the weight I've been carrying, it's just not sustainable.'

He nodded. 'That's not uncommon for fast-paced, high-achieving leaders like you. And recognising it *before* burnout hits – that's a gift.'

'Exactly. If I'm going to finish well and stay the course, something has to change.'

Tom leaned in. 'And this will lead to more fruitful ministry – as you step back and let God take the lead.'

His words landed. I paused, then shared what had been stirring in me.

'There's a scripture that's been speaking to me lately – and I think it's going to be foundational for the whole sabbatical: "Come to me, all you who are weary and burdened, and I will give you rest . . . For my yoke is easy and my burden is light."'[22]

Tom smiled. 'And at the heart of that easy yoke is pace and direction.'

22. Matthew 11:28–30

As the call ended, his words stayed with me. I knew I was heading in the right direction – but I needed to find a better rhythm. One led not by pressure, but by presence. I was ready to enter this sabbatical rest.

When I brought it to the Board, they gave their full support. It was set for the following summer.

***

'Tom, I know the primary purpose of my sabbatical is rest and deepening my relationship with God, and it's been absolutely amazing,' I said during one of our sabbatical check-ins. 'But I'm also learning so much from a couple of books I've been reading. And the funny thing is, they're confirming things you've been saying to me for years! I just wasn't ready to fully take them on board before. But now? Oh, I'm ready!' I leaned forward, a grin spreading across my face.

Tom smiled, eyes twinkling. 'And what's that, Ricky?'

'Well, first off, I'm realising how "being" leads to more effective "doing" – and how I had it completely backwards. Yes, I always invested in my relationship with God, but if I'm honest, it was often secondary to my service for him.'

Tom's face lit up. 'I'm so glad this is finally landing for you! Because the irony is, when we get out of the way and let God lead – when intimacy with him becomes our first priority – our ministry actually bears more fruit, not less.'

I chuckled and shook my head. 'Tom, I wish I'd grasped this earlier! Maybe I wouldn't have worn myself out so much. But I guess sometimes the only way we learn is through the school of hard knocks.'

We both laughed, but then Tom's tone grew more serious. 'This is exactly why someone like you – so driven, so focused – needs to learn to be led by God rather than lead from your drivenness. The impact of this shift on you, your ministry, and your team will be huge.'

I sat with his words for a moment, then nodded slowly. 'You're right. And now that I've slowed down enough to reflect, I'm beginning to see the effect my pace has had – not just on me, but on those around me.' I lowered my head and exhaled. 'I've pushed hard for so long – too hard.'

'Don't be too hard on yourself,' Tom said gently. 'As a high D on the DISC profile myself, I get it. That's why we connect so well – we speak the same language. The key is, you're recognising this now, before it's too late. Far too many leaders wait until they've hit burnout.'

I nodded again, quieter this time. 'Yeah, I know a few who have.'

A thoughtful silence lingered between us, the weight of reality settling in.

'Another key lesson I'm processing,' I added, 'is the role of adversity – how God uses hardship to deepen our dependence on him.'

Tom leaned in. 'That's a hard one – but vital to grasp.'

'Yeah,' I said, my voice more measured now. 'I've been reflecting on how God's used the challenges of the past few years to shape me. I wouldn't have chosen those trials, but I can't deny how he's worked through them. It's humbling.'

Tom smiled warmly. 'Ricky, all of this is forming you – refining you for what's ahead. This is spiritual growth worth celebrating.'

I grinned. 'We definitely should celebrate it. And one final lesson I'm learning? Timing. I've often been good at sensing direction, but I've been terrible at waiting.'

Tom laughed. 'Waiting on God's timing is going to stretch you – no doubt. But if you truly keep prioritising "being over doing", you'll get there. Trust me.'

Looking back, these sabbatical lessons would prove to be life-changing. What I'd initially seen as time away from work became one of the most transformative decisions of my life – not just for me, but for the future of Street Connect.

***

As I prepared to step back into 'normal life', my thoughts turned once more to Street Connect and the road ahead. The sabbatical hadn't just refreshed me, it had reshaped me. I was returning with a renewed clarity: if we were to move into the next season of growth, we had to do it differently.

One of the key principles guiding us forward was simple but profound: less is more. After three years of intense development, it was time to streamline. Growth wasn't about doing more; it was about doing what mattered most, at the right time, with the right people. I now understood that fruitfulness comes not from striving, but from abiding.

Now, we weren't just dreaming of national reach, we were poised to step into it – not from a place of pressure, but from a place of peace.

But vision alone wouldn't carry us. We had to care for the people entrusted with it. If we were serious about leading differently, it had to begin with our culture. We reduced the working week from 37.5 to 35 hours, increased salaries and annual leave, and made a conscious decision to prioritise soul care across the organisation. Burnout wasn't inevitable – and we were determined it wouldn't be our story.

With those foundations in place, the stage was set. Street Connect wasn't just expanding – we were stepping into a healthier, more sustainable rhythm of leadership. The shift from regional to national wasn't just a strategic move. It was the fruit of a deeper transformation – one rooted in listening, stillness, and the quiet conviction that God leads best when we learn to follow – if we're still enough to hear his voice.

Conclusion

Not Finished Yet: National Expansion

It is 'for such a time as this[23] *that I am raising up the work of Street Connect.*

The words echoed in my heart as the latest drug death statistics for Scotland were announced – still, by far, the highest in Europe. Nearly three times higher than anywhere else in the UK or Europe.

I sat back in my chair, the weight of it all pressing down on me.

This is it, I thought. *This is why God brought me to Glasgow. Why he planted Street Connect in the very heart of the city with the highest drug death rate – not just in Scotland, but across the entire UK and Europe.*

23. Esther 4:14.

Thank you, God, I whispered, struck by the clarity of his plan.

Looking back now, I could see it – how he'd been guiding every step, even when I hadn't known it. This is why we have the team we do. This is why we're rooted right here. Because God loves this city. He loves the people in it – a city where even the streets cry out for hope . . .

***

'Let's go down this alleyway – and be prepared . . .' one of our intern project workers said during outreach. He'd once been supported by Street Connect himself and, after completing rehab, knew every injecting site in Glasgow city centre like the back of his hand.

That day, we were joined by a team from a major evening news outlet. They wanted a glimpse of the reality on the ground, especially as Glasgow prepared to launch the UK's first ever drug consumption facility.

We stepped off one of the city's busiest streets and made our way down the alley. 'Let's set up there for the interview,' the cameraman said, pointing to a spot next to a steel bin fixed to the ground – strategically placed for disposing of used needles.

Within seconds, the harsh reality began to unfold.

Just off to the side, two women were injecting behind a parked car. A man who looked every bit the part of a street dealer scanned the alley, eyes darting.

Before we could process what we were seeing, a voice cut through the air. 'What are you all doing here?'

A homeless man stepped towards us, his face weathered, eyes tired.

'I've been living down that side street for two years since getting out of prison,' he said. 'Safer there than in the hostels. It's dog-eat-dog out here. I'm always having to fight folk off trying to steal my money or my gear.'

As he spoke, another man walked past, holding a loaded needle, scanning for a quiet spot. Dirty needles littered the pavement. More people came and went, weaving in and out like shadows.

We'd only been there ten, maybe fifteen minutes.

I'd seen a lot over the years – in my own addiction and in this line of work – but even I was moved. I turned and looked back up the alleyway, less than a hundred yards away. Crowds bustled past – shoppers, office workers, tourists – all oblivious. Just moments from this hidden world.

Later, back in my office, the moment hit me hard.

This is why we're here.

This is why our regional expansion matters.

God has a plan for his Church in this city and the surrounding areas, and we're called to play our part in tackling this crisis head-on.

'Right, let's get the stuff to the car,' I said to Julie as we packed up our bags, ready for the long drive back to Glasgow. It was 5:30 a.m. – early by most people's standards, but we're definitely morning people. We'd just finished a fruitful conference in Birmingham and needed to get home in time for the kids.

As we made our way around the side of the hotel in the heart of the city, our eyes were drawn to a group of six people lying on flattened cardboard and blankets, tucked beside the building.

'Good morning,' I said gently as we passed by.

Once we reached the car, Julie paused. 'I'm going to get a few of the Street Connect testimony booklets and some of our cards to give them,' she said, already turning back.

She crouched down. 'Hi, how are you this morning? Can I give you one of these?'

Before we knew it, we were each in conversation with different people.

'So who are you?' asked one of the men, his face weathered by years of hardship. There was a guarded edge in his voice, like someone always braced for disappointment.

'We're from a charity called Street Connect,' I replied. 'We support people struggling with addiction and related challenges.'

'I'm not sleeping rough,' he said quickly. 'I'm in one of the hostels around the corner. Just out of prison.'

Before he could finish, a softer voice called out.

'Can you help us?' asked another man, open and childlike. He said he was staying in a tent nearby with his best friend, who sat slumped behind him.

'That's him there,' he said. 'He got jumped last night by a couple of young guys.'

The first man's voice cut in again, sharp. 'If I get my hands on them . . .'

But the second gently touched my arm and leaned in. His eyes were wide, searching.

'Can you help me?' he asked again, his voice cracking.

'With what?'

'My life's a mess,' he said, eyes dropping. 'I need to do something. I'll do anything.'

We stepped aside to talk. I explained what we do and how we could support him. As I spoke, something shifted in his face. His eyes welled up, and a tear rolled down his cheek.

'It's my birthday today,' he whispered. 'And this . . . this is the best present I could hope for.'

There it was – in just a few minutes, the hopelessness had been cracked open by something stronger. Hope. You could see it in his eyes. There was such a hunger for more.

I handed him a card. 'Call this number. We'll connect you with one of our support workers. You're not on your own.'

'Can you get us a hot drink?' one of the girls called out.

'And some breakfast too!' the first man added with a cheeky grin.

Julie and I glanced at each other and laughed.

'You're pushing it now – but we like your style,' I replied.

We spent nearly an hour with the group before heading home.

Back in the car, I stared out the window as the motorway slipped past. My thoughts drifted from the streets of Birmingham to the stories we'd heard at the conference – and suddenly, one moment stood out clear in my mind . . .

***

Back at the conference the previous day, I had just sat down during a moment of reflection. I had spoken earlier about the work of Street Connect – how, in a nutshell, we take people from the street, to their feet, to a life complete.

As I settled into my seat, a pastor I knew walked by, then quietly took the seat behind mine. As he did, I felt his hand rest gently on my shoulder. He leaned in and whispered words that hit like an arrow to the heart.

'You're a father to the fatherless,' he said softly, 'and many will come back to the Father through you.'

My heart burned. I knew this wasn't just a kind encouragement – it was a divine confirmation. A moment of clarity. In that instant, I sensed God placing his mantle more firmly on my shoulders – not just for those in Glasgow and the surrounding area, but for the nation.

Now, sitting beside Julie, watching the city fade into the distance behind us, I could feel the weight and wonder of that word all over again. And the timing. Drug-related deaths in England and Wales were at their highest since records began. Alcohol deaths were no better. And the wider impact on society was undeniable.

God wasn't finished with me. He wasn't finished with us.

The streets of Birmingham, the alleyways of Glasgow, the cries of those lost in addiction – each one a fresh reminder. And it's not just the major cities. The towns. Rural communities. All are affected by the destructive reach of addiction. But what do they all have in common?

Churches.

Each of these places has churches embedded within their communities – local expressions of God's heart – who can play a vital role in tackling this crisis.

Looking ahead, I wanted a simple way to test the principle I'd learned: that the best leadership flows from getting out of the way and letting God take the lead. So at the end of each year, I ask myself three questions:

> Are we reaching and supporting more people?
>
> Are we equipping more churches?
>
> And is our income increasing to enable the first two?

Year after year, the answer to each has been a resounding yes. For me, it's more than a performance review; it's confirmation that when we abide, he truly does bear the fruit, in his way and in his time.

I remain amazed at how far God has brought me – from a life of brokenness and addiction to leading a movement of hope across the nation. But this isn't the end of the story. It's just another beginning. The journey has never been about me. It's always been about him – his power to redeem, his heart for the lost, and his call to each of us to say yes.

My part is simply to keep showing up, keep listening, and keep following. Because the work's not finished yet – and neither am I.

Join Us In Bringing Hope and Transformation

At Street Connect, we believe no life is beyond hope. My own journey from addiction to freedom is proof of that. Every day, our team works alongside individuals and communities across the UK to help people move from the street, to their feet, to a life complete.

We are stepping into an exciting new ten-year vision: to grow from a regional ministry into a nationwide movement. By 2036, our aim is to see a hundred church partner locations supported by five regional hubs across the UK – giving thousands more people the chance to find freedom, restoration, and hope.

You can be part of this mission:

Give – Your donations help us reach and support more people in need.

Partner – Churches can join us in bringing lasting transformation to their communities.

Volunteer – Your time, skills, and compassion can make a life-changing difference.

Pray – Lift the work of Street Connect and those we serve before God in prayer.

Scan the QR code to donate now or find out more.

Website:	www.streetconnect.co.uk
Email:	info@streetconnect.co.uk
Facebook:	facebook.com/streetconnectuk
Instagram:	instagram.com/streetconnectuk
X (Twitter):	twitter.com/streetconnectuk

Together, we can see lives transformed – one life at a time.

Acknowledgements

I must begin by thanking God. Without his intervention, this book would never have been written, and Street Connect would not exist – at least not with me as part of it. Far more importantly, the trajectory and eternal destination of my life would be entirely different. I dare not imagine where I'd be now without him. He is my everything.

Secondly, I thank my family for never giving up on me. Even through my years of chaos, you stood by me. I am forever grateful for your undying love and support.

Thank you to everyone who contributed to this book – your input has greatly enriched its content. In particular, I'm grateful to Julie, Peter Vincent, Alistair Matheson, Alex Nicol, Jamie, and Charlie for sharing their stories and perspectives, portions of which appear throughout these pages. My thanks also to Liz Dobson, Ali Hull and Lorna Farrell for their early guidance when my writing was far from polished;

to Anthony Gielty, whose redrafting and creative input across several early sections and other scenes helped refine the narrative voice and strengthen the flow of the book; and to Sheila Jacobs for both of your editorial reports – the first was hard to take, but invaluable in sharpening the final manuscript. Thanks also to the Board of Trustees for allowing me to write this book during work hours. Without that support, I doubt it would have been completed.

I'm grateful to all my mentors over the years, each of whom has played a role in shaping the man I am today. Thank you to Teen Challenge for taking me in and giving me another chance; to King's Church Ilford for loving me; and to Glasgow City Church – especially Peter Vincent – for believing in Julie and me.

To Julie: thank you for journeying with me on this God adventure. I'm truly thankful for you and our four children – you mean the world to me.

Finally, to all who have played a part in the mission of Street Connect since its formation: I would have loved to name every one of you, but there are simply too many! You know who you are, and, more importantly, God knows. So a heartfelt thank you to all our staff and volunteers, supporters and funders, partners and friends. None of this would have been possible without your dedication and support.

www.ingramcontent.com/pod-product-compliance
Lightning Source LLC
LaVergne TN
LVHW020042110826
845155LV00029B/595
* 9 7 8 1 9 1 7 4 5 5 4 8 0 *